FIELD
OF
DREAMS

FIELD
OF
DREAMS

BOB SALISBURY

·THE·
BLACK
·STAFF
PRESS

To those dedicated to giving wildlife a chance

First published in 2018 by Blackstaff Press
an imprint of Colourpoint Creative Ltd, Colourpoint House,
Jubilee Business Park, 21 Jubilee Road,
Newtownards, BT23 4YH

With the assistance of The Arts Council of Northern Ireland

LOTTERY FUNDED

Printed in Berwick-upon-Tweed by Martins the Printers

A CIP catalogue for this book is available from the British Library

ISBN 978 1 78073 172 8

www.blackstaffpress.com

Contents

Prologue 1

1 The Idea 3

2 Making a Start 28

3 Water 49

4 The Wild Garden 66

5 More Formal Moves 83

6 First Arrivals 98

7 More Newcomers 115

8 Fresh Pastures 138

9 Moving On 155

10 Winning Ways 167

Acknowledgements 186

Prologue

It was when we first spent time on the land we had just bought in County Tyrone that Rosemary asked me a question.

'Do you notice anything odd?'

After a series of guesses I gave up.

'Well, we are sitting here in the Irish countryside but there is no birdsong. Nothing is moving, except for a few rooks in the distance. When I was growing up here there were skylarks, butterflies, partridge and all kinds of small birds, and at this time of year we could always hear curlews over there on the bogland. Where have they all gone? It's like a rural desert!'

Rosemary was absolutely right and, even when I scanned the surroundings with binoculars, there was still no sign of anything. What a contrast with our old garden in Sherwood Forest where we could always see something to delight the senses. For many years we had both enjoyed the moments when we spotted some bird or animal that was extra special – roding woodcock, sparrow hawks, three kinds of owl and, on one occasion, a nightjar.

We had chosen country living in Ireland in large part because of our interest in birds and wild creatures, and it came as a shock to realise that the land seemed to be so devoid of life. Rosemary noticed the disappointment on my face and said, 'We're going to have to make some kind of garden here and perhaps we should try to create an area that is attractive to wildlife and see what turns up. Something must live around here and, as the experts say, if we get the habitat right, maybe the birds and animals will come back.'

So that was how the idea was born. Fourteen years ago we began a project that has since become totally absorbing and deeply satisfying – the creation of our wildlife garden.

1
The Idea

Rosemary knew that there had once been wildlife on our newly acquired plot because she had been born in a house just over the nearest hill and her father once owned the land on which we now sat. He had been killed in a tractor accident on the farm in 1951 when she was eighteen months old and for years the fields had been rented out to people who had little long-term interest in maintaining or improving the land. Much of it was now sadly neglected. At eighteen Rosemary had left for England in order to become a teacher and had ended up staying for thirty-three years. 'Must have been a pretty tough course,' some wit once said, but actually we had met and married in 1975, bought an old gamekeeper's cottage on the edge of Sherwood Forest, and developed the garden and house into a delightful home. The reasons we opted for rural living rather than buying a property in the town, which would have been much more convenient (especially once children came along), were because of influences lodged deep in both our psyches.

In my case, I was brought up in a nondescript street that had twenty semi-detached houses with tiny gardens, on the edge of a small industrial town in Nottinghamshire. This was part of a spreading urban area, but the gardens of the houses at the bottom end of the street opened out into farmland, woodlands and long-established country lanes. I felt I was growing up in two worlds: go to the top of the street and look left down the hill and a sprawl of factories, railway sidings, shops and pubs stretched into the distance. A smoke pall always hung over the town and the railway shunting yards and the clatter of machines reverberated through the streets, day and night. The town had grown in all directions with new housing developments, industrial parks and road networks continually encroaching on the landscape.

But if I turned right at the top of the street, the road led to butterfly meadows, ivy-clad cottages, ancient farmhouses, rivers with fish and bracken-covered hillsides. Ageing orchards protected by thick hawthorn hedges were everywhere and, in the fruiting season, we were happy to scramble through the thorns to reach the abundant supplies of pears, apples and plums. The contrast was stark and as early as I can remember I was always drawn instinctively to the countryside.

It is difficult to imagine now the freedom given to children in the early fifties: on non-school days or summer evenings I roamed endlessly, getting to know every inch of the land. Supervision was minimal, money unnecessary and my regular routes frequently took me away from home for hours to return at the end of the day thirsty, scratched, filthy and exhausted but thoroughly happy. My appetite for learning about the creatures and plants that I saw on these excursions was boundless and marked the beginning of a love of the countryside that has never left me.

Rosemary's outlook was somewhat different. Living in Ireland following her father's death was tough going. The farm produced very little in rent and getting by from week to week was always a balancing act with nothing left for any kind of luxury. She hated the fact that much of their land was neglected and unproductive, and growing up she saw no beauty in the farmland that yielded only hardship and poverty. 'Land has to be cherished, nurtured, looked after – they're not making any more of it!' she would say. Developing our garden in Sherwood Forest and cultivating the small field that came with it was part of this passionate philosophy.

We reared three fine sons as the years flew by. The boys finally moved on for study and employment and were doing well. Rosemary's career also prospered. Opportunities for advancement in schools in England were about talent, vision and commitment, in contrast to what we heard about Northern Ireland, where long service or patronage often still seemed to hold sway. Having taken ten years out to bring up the children, Rosemary eventually became head teacher of a large secondary school in Retford, Nottinghamshire, and getting this post was quite a coup. The school had been founded in 1552 and the oak plaques lining the great hall listed the names of every head teacher since then. Rosemary was the first woman principal.

I had also been a head teacher and had moved on to work as a professor in the School of Education at the University of Nottingham when two things happened that changed the direction of our lives.

The first was that Rosemary discovered, in the first few weeks of 2001, that she was in the early stages of breast cancer. A small burn at the base of her right thumb that failed to heal and the tiny dimple she had noticed on her breast prompted her to go for a health check. Within days she was being operated on to have a small but malignant tumour removed. Luckily it was diagnosed and treated early and the prognosis from the medics was positive and optimistic.

The second significant event was when Bernadette Grant, one of Rosemary's old teachers from Ireland, wrote out of the blue to say that the Integrated College in Omagh, County Tyrone, was looking for a new principal. In her view it required someone of Rosemary's experience and vision to 'shake it up'! The rigid, sectarian nature of schools in Northern Ireland had always seemed to us to sit in direct opposition to the educational principles we believed in and Rosemary felt that leading the college might in some small way help to contribute towards a much-needed change in culture.

As my role in the School of Education took me to all parts of the UK, and flying was relatively cheap and easy, we decided to move to Ireland when Rosemary was offered the post. Initially, I don't think we regarded the move as permanent – more that it would be an interesting change for a few years at least. In addition, as a keen fisherman the country certainly held serious attraction for me!

We decided as a starting point to test out the market by putting our cottage up for sale. It was situated seven miles from the centre of Nottingham on the edge of Sherwood Forest. We had created a wonderful retreat inside its attractive walled garden, had established an orchard, and knew that its distinctive architecture and positioning would make it a desirable property. We were right – it sold almost immediately for the asking price – so we were very soon fully committed to a move to Ireland, although at that stage we still felt it would be a short-term stay.

We had of course visited Ireland many times on holiday but being a tourist in any country is not the same as living there. So, once we thought it might become permanent, we had some mixed feelings about the move. We were aware that Northern Ireland had areas of breathtaking, unspoiled countryside where the lakelands, coasts and mountains were spectacular and the countryside was seldom crowded. We knew also that the air was clean, the roads relatively empty and the cost of living comparatively cheap. It seemed a very appealing place to live but we were not naive enough to think that the divisions in the society, which had led to so much bloodshed in the past, would be easily healed.

We had an old friend, a retired school inspector, who lived in Northern Ireland and he reinforced a lot of what we already appreciated: that Northern Ireland was a lovely place to live with very low crime rates, especially in the kinds of rural areas we were looking at. Knowing Rosemary was from Tyrone, he recommended it as the perfect county for us – within range of the Fermanagh lakelands, the beautiful beaches of Donegal and the Sperrin mountains, and Derry and Belfast within an hour's drive. But he had a warning for us: 'Never listen to the phone-in programmes on the radio – they always seem to attract the worst kinds of sectarian bigots, talentless politicians and people who want to blame the whole world for ills of their own making.'

I never did work out whether he was joking or serious about the advice he gave!

Rosemary left for Ireland in early August 2001 to take up her new post and I stayed behind to complete the house sale and to sort out thirty years of accumulated possessions. We packed some, sold off others, and the rest simply went to charity shops. What is it that makes us store worthless junk in the hope that 'it may come in useful one day'? We'd filled three skips before the house and garage were finally cleared.

Once the paperwork was signed I set off, driving behind two furniture vans towards our new life. To begin with, the journey was slow, tedious and uneventful. Moving at fifty-five miles an hour along a motorway is frustrating to say the least and it was a relief when we finally stopped for a break at a motorway service station. Just inside the entrance a knot of people were silently staring at a television set mounted on the wall. There was clearly tension in the air and I asked the nearest person what was happening.

His reply shocked me. 'A plane has hit one of the Twin Towers in New York.'

'A private plane?' I asked.

'No an airliner – it looks like terrorism.'

For the next hour or so I totally forgot about our move and watched in horror as the events on 11 September 2001 unfolded. Back on the road the world suddenly seemed a much more dangerous place.

We found a house to rent near Rosemary's school and immediately set about touring Fermanagh and Tyrone, looking for a place to buy. It was more problematic than we had anticipated. The older properties often occupied superb sites beside rivers or lakes, and had mature gardens with spectacular specimen trees. They were also astonishingly well priced but were seriously lacking in modern amenities. The Irish climate plays havoc with timber, plaster and roofing and many of the houses we visited were damp and dismal. Often these old buildings and homes that were once occupied by people of status were nothing more than decaying heaps with obsolete electrics, inadequate heating, leaky roofs and rotting window frames. Many looked like they had been badly constructed in the first place as second-division aristos tried to emulate their wealthier cousins by building cut-price versions of 'such-and-such hall' or 'somewhere house'. The established drives and gardens still suggested places of grandeur, but behind the facades lurked the smell of decay and peeling plaster.

Oddly enough, some had retained vestiges of their former status within their local communities, even though they were falling apart, and people still referred to them as 'the big house' or 'the hall'. Prestige they may have had but bringing them up to any kind of acceptable standard would be a never-ending project. We had spent the first years of our married life renovating the cottage in Sherwood Forest and though we loved the end result, we knew just how much effort has to go into making this kind of property fit for the twenty-first century. Taking on that kind of challenge the first time was in many ways a youthful adventure, but we felt that tackling one of these crumbling country houses now would be nothing short of a life sentence.

Newer properties appeared to be very good value in terms of their size and amenities, especially compared to the rest of the UK. It was clear that the finance raised from the sale of our cottage would purchase considerably more land or property than it would have done in England. But unfortunately many of the newer houses were just not to our taste. Properties were often badly positioned next to busy roads, or designed in a way that we felt was at odds with their surroundings. Texan ranch houses, Mexican haciendas and timber-faced mock Tudor mansions obviously appealed to their owners but did not seem to us to sit easily in the rural landscape. One especially odd local effort, built at the confluence of two rivers, was designed like a fairy-tale castle with turrets, Gothic windows and towers. It must have cost a small fortune to build but looked like a leftover from a Disney film set and was totally out of place in its exceptional riverside setting.

There were some really attractive traditional Irish houses, rectangular in shape with stone quoins and roofs of blue slate that were at one with the landscape, but many had been built in drab and uninspiring locations, which was particularly hard to understand given the abundance of beautiful countryside. One local man explained to us that these were often sites on farmland given to family members – odd corners of the farm that would not affect its running, rather than well-situated plots. A free site is a free site, though, so the houses went up.

The small single-storey stone cottages, which for centuries were traditional across Ireland, have been steadily replaced by their modern equivalent – block-built bungalows. Though architecturally a little dull, these dwellings were originally not intrusive as they usually sat on mature sites and reflected the size and shape of the original buildings. Unfortunately, though, in some outstandingly scenic areas, regulation appears to have been slack and a planning free-for-all over the last thirty years has led to a second home 'bungalow blight' that has changed magnificent wild places into semi-deserted, grubby holiday suburbs. This was particularly noticeable on some slopes overlooking the sea where uncontrolled building has transformed truly spectacular natural landscapes into what look from a distance like the crowded properties on a Monopoly board.

I enquired of one planner how decisions were made about planning approval and his response was puzzling. 'We try to encourage a traditional Irish style that will not be too obtrusive on the landscape and will still be acceptable in twenty years or so.'

This reasoning did not seem to equate with what has been built in places and, as one cynic suggested, perhaps with tongue in cheek, maybe acceptable style depends on who gets the brown envelope and how much is in it!

What made matters worse was that developers seemed to have the notion that felling all existing trees and grubbing out ancient hedgerows was necessary before any building could begin. Of course some roadside clearance is necessary to meet sightline regulations but the total removal of the existing trees and hedges seemed excessive. It meant completed houses stood out like sore thumbs and, for people interested in privacy and conservation as we were, these scoured building sites were hardly inviting.

This total clearance of building sites struck me as so odd that when I bumped into a local craftsman who had constructed many houses in the area, I couldn't resist asking him more about the reasons.

'People who build a new house want it to be seen by those who pass by,' he told me. 'Hiding it behind hedges or trees is not what the majority demand so we take the vegetation from the site and make the property stand out.'

I pointed out that many of the houses were a real blot on the landscape and certainly didn't sit easily in their surroundings, especially in the rural areas.

'That's a matter of opinion,' he said carefully. 'As builders we just try to satisfy the demand.'

Ironically, the tree cover that had been cleared often gave the new dwellings their names. So where there was once a splendid cherry tree, the building became Cherry Tree Cottage, the beech wood that was felled gave its name to Beech View and the ancient sycamore that was axed prompted the truly aspirational Sycamore House.

As we got to know the country, our choice seemed clear: to buy a house in need of renovation with mature gardens or to go for a new build and begin the garden from scratch. However, a chance conversation with an estate agent changed our thinking. 'Land is very cheap at the moment and you will be able to purchase far more for much less than you would pay for a similar acreage in England. Farmers are releasing building sites and planning is much more relaxed than across the water. There are plenty of potential plots and you should be able to find a couple of acres in the right setting where you could build a modern property that will blend in. Materials and labour costs are reasonable and you could have the whole thing designed and built in a couple of years.'

This seemed like a way forward and we tried to narrow down the criteria for the kind of plot that would suit our needs. We felt it should be in undulating or hilly countryside – which would have interest both in the foreground and at a distance – and that it would have to offer privacy. Much of the centre of Northern Ireland is flat so we concentrated on Tyrone and Fermanagh where landscapes are more scenic and varied. We were very tempted by sites on the lower slopes of the Sperrins as there were spectacular views – particularly from some of the more prominent peaks, where, on a clear day, it was possible to see the distant mountains of Donegal. Though these locations were inviting when the weather was calm, we soon learned that the picture changed dramatically when the winter storms blew in from the Atlantic. One particular site, which seemed ideal on the calm sunny day we first saw it, was transformed into a gardener's nightmare when the westerly gales blew.

'It would be difficult to grow anything but gorse here with this wind,' Rosemary said, leaning forward into the powerful gusts, 'and any washing out on a line would probably finish up in Scotland.'

One thing we were certain about was that whatever site we eventually chose would not be anywhere near a main road, and that we would build the house itself at the end of a long drive. Sustained traffic noise carries for miles in certain weather conditions and its intrusion can totally spoil the peace of any rural setting. Furthermore, being too close to the road can sometimes prove hazardous, as we discovered on more than one occasion when we lived in England.

It was the year 1993 and it started well enough. Every summer we left for a month on the continent with a trailer tent, caravan or – on this particular occasion – a motor caravan. Luckily we had listened to the advice of the salesman who had recommended that we should buy the motor home with the reinforced steel frame at the back, in spite of the additional expense, as it was so much safer. After a superb holiday in the Harz Mountains we crossed back to England on the early ferry and decided to rest up for a while in a large lay-by some twenty metres away from the main road.

We had barely got to sleep when a tremendous explosion rocked the van and brought cupboards, pots and side panels crashing down. Pain seared through my whole body and for a few seconds I was paralysed and could not move my hands or feet. I thought initially that a gas cylinder had somehow exploded but then realised that a hot engine was a few inches from my head and that someone had crashed into us. Petrol was running down into my mouth and I could see through the steam and the wreckage that it was spurting from a fuel pump that was still working. A bloodied, bemused face appeared in the shattered windscreen.

'Turn your ignition off,' I yelled, trying to get up to see the driver.

'Lie still! Don't move! You might have damaged your spine,' said Rosemary, using more common sense. 'I'll get help.'

She had been sleeping at the front of the camper van along with the two older boys and mercifully all three were uninjured. Howard, our youngest, had been lying next to me and had been shielded from most of the impact by my body but still suffered chipped teeth and minor injuries.

Police and emergency services were quickly on the scene, and as I was being removed from the wreckage, I heard one fireman say, 'The steel frame on the back of this van definitely saved these folks – that's for sure. Look at the metal embedded in that cushion.'

The driver – who it turned out was drunk, already banned from driving and in a stolen car – was arrested. He later served a prison sentence.

I was gently strapped to a stretcher and whisked off to Addenbrooke's Hospital in Cambridge. Luckily, a top spinal specialist was in the hospital preparing a talk for later in the day and he examined me. He ascertained that the sixth vertebra was broken but he said encouragingly, 'You may get lucky and we should be able to fix it.'

I was tightly trussed up and placed in a side ward. Every few hours a six-person team came, lifted me and turned me round a few degrees, like a pig being roasted on a barbecue. I was issued with prismatic glasses to make reading or watching television possible whilst lying flat on my back, but the days seemed endless. One welcome break to the monotony came when a nurse informed me that I could at last try some solid food. She placed oxtail soup and a finely shredded salad on a bed tray over my chest and disappeared. The dexterity required to eat either of these whilst lying flat and peering through prisms would test the skills of the most able NASA astronaut so I had no chance. Within minutes the pillows and bed looked like a muddy compost heap. I wondered why they didn't just bring me a sandwich.

A few weeks later, wearing a stiff plastic collar and neck scaffolding, I got up a little too quickly from my chair at home, pushed off with my arm and managed to dislocate my right shoulder. This was an old rugby injury and I was very familiar with the pain and the likely treatment. Rosemary rushed me to the local hospital and, as I was being wheeled down to the theatre, a nurse saw me smiling and said, 'Most people are not too happy going along this corridor. What do you find so amusing?'

'I can't believe I am going under the lights again. It seems only minutes since I was there.'

Two nights on, now sporting the plastic collar, the neck scaffolding and a sling on my right arm, a dull thump reverberated through the cottage. It felt like something heavy had fallen upstairs. The doorbell went and a teenage girl and her brother stood there looking visibly shaken.

'I've just spun off the road and crashed into your garage.'

'Is anyone hurt?' I asked, acting like a benevolent uncle.

'No, we are both okay.'

'Don't worry,' I said. 'Everything can be sorted out.'

But when I turned on the light in the garage, a scene of devastation faced us. The girl's car had demolished the gable end and had wedged itself into the side of my three-litre pride and joy. Bricks and rubble covered the bonnet and roof, and nails and tools that had been fired from the workbench were embedded in the panels. Rosemary's car fared little better and looked like it had been in a bomb blast.

I am ashamed to say that I then metamorphosed from a benevolent uncle to a ranting loon. Haranguing an eighteen year old after she had wrecked her car and been in her first accident was definitely not my finest hour, but standing there in neck brace and sling, after the last few weeks, I felt I'd reached my limit.

In two months we had gone from never making a claim to calling on our health insurance, and claiming for major repairs to three vehicles, the rebuilding of the garage and the replacement of the equipment and contents in the garage. The only policy we didn't need to use was the household pet insurance. When I phoned the various companies it was not 'Do you have a policy number, Mr Salisbury?' but 'Hi Bob! How are things going? Dogs still okay?'

★

We persevered in our search for a site – far from a busy road – and our introduction to price negotiation in Ireland was an education in itself. When the people selling the land heard my English accent they automatically assumed we had benefited from the astronomical sums properties in England were fetching at that time. A typical conversation went like this:

'Have you sold a place in England?' the farmer would ask.

'Yes.'

'How much land are you after?'

'An acre or so, running down to the river.'

'You could have this piece here for sixty grand,' and his arm would sweep vaguely in the direction of the watercourse.

I was still considering the possibilities after one such conversation as the farmer and Rosemary continued to saunter through the field. She chatted to him about where she had grown up, her father's accident and the fact that neither of us had come from privileged backgrounds. She went on to say that when we first married our only possessions were a bed and a fridge; that we had had to work hard to bring up our three boys; and that just because we'd sold a house in England didn't mean we were loaded. As we reached our car and were climbing back into it, Rosemary told him how much she had enjoyed talking to him and almost incidentally asked how much he'd said he wanted for the site. Without any apparent embarrassment the farmer replied, 'At a push I could come down to thirty.' That's negotiation for you!

Eventually we found a possible site on land that was once owned by Rosemary's father. We were taken by the attractive, hilly countryside that had unspoiled views to the south, and a border of mature ash trees on the northern and western sides. Most importantly, much of the land lay on the leeward side of a ridge and was largely sheltered from the worst of the winter gales. In addition, though we had never thought about it beforehand, purchasing this land just seemed right. It was as if we were destined to restore these acres to the family. Rosemary's father had worked hard to reclaim acres of marginal land into a workable farm and it seemed fitting that his efforts should live on and hopefully prosper under our stewardship.

'It's high time these fields came back to their rightful owners,' said one elderly cousin. 'This has always been family land.'

The downside was that the land had been neglected for many years and much of it was reed-covered and waterlogged, with drainage ditches overgrown and clogged. Scenically, the place had great potential but the original site was too small and much too close to the road. Fortunately, there was the possibility of buying a larger plot.

We duly submitted a design for outline planning approval because without it there would be little point proceeding. The design included, mainly with future saleability in mind, a rudimentary idea of what the garden might look like. Much to our surprise – because planning permission famously takes ages – approval came through almost at once. The planner who phoned with the news said, 'We really liked the fact that you submitted plans to enhance the land around the property and are considering making this a requirement for all submissions in the future.' With this endorsement we agreed to buy the land – but establishing title and getting the deeds signed over was a frustrating business and seemed to take forever. Finally, though, we owned a five-acre piece of Irish countryside. Just getting to this stage had taken nearly two years.

It was then, when we were finally able to spend time on the land that was ours, that Rosemary noticed the complete absence of any birds or wildlife. It had certainly not been this empty when she was growing up – she remembered skylarks, curlews, partridge, dozens of small birds, and the air alive with butterflies. For the first time, we started to think more about our plans for the garden and knew that whatever we did, our starting point would be to try to attract the birds and animals back.

Obviously we knew that however successful our efforts in this tiny corner of Tyrone became, we could never counteract the widespread devastation of wildlife that has occurred across the UK in only two generations and that we were now witnessing first hand. In some small way we were committed to trying to reverse the trend but, looking at the land as it was, our dream was a daunting prospect. As armchair conservationists, it is easy to see that we should be more aware of preserving what we have and looking after valuable habitats for those who come after, but in practical terms it is also very easy to feel powerless in the face of relentless 'progress'. However we firmly believed that, if this project worked, it might have a little influence locally, and could eventually lead us to a different attitude towards managing our land and gardens. As the Dalai Lama once said, 'If you think you are too small to make a difference, try sleeping with a mosquito.'

Even at the beginning, we knew that it wouldn't be easy. The wet land was a good example of where resilience was required. After any prolonged rainfall, it would become completely waterlogged and virtually impassable, with surface water lying everywhere. Designing a more diverse habitat sometimes seemed hardly achievable at all. One damp morning I was cutting back some brambles on the roadside, when a farmer rattled up on a mud-spattered quad. His sheep, with their distinctive blue markings, were in the field next to where I stood and he stopped to check the flock. He was short and wiry and jumping from his machine, strode across for a chat.

'Not a bad day,' he said and I nodded and went on to introduce myself. He was called Darren but, as he informed me with a grin, everyone called him Daz.

'I used to roam all over the land when I was a boy and knew every corner of it. We often avoided the fields you've bought because in wet weather it was hard going and easy to get bogged down. The mud would pull at the boots so we preferred to stay on the higher ground.'

'We hope to try to create a kind of wildlife garden here,' I said.

'Good luck to ye,' he replied, as he fired up the ancient machine and disappeared noisily over the hill.

As newcomers to the area, we were interested in finding out what had happened to the ecology Rosemary remembered from her childhood so decided to go over to Seskinore Forest to see Jim Whiteside. He is a retired forester and wildlife expert, now in his eighties, who is known across Northern Ireland for his work in preserving rare poultry breeds, hand rearing of grouse and championing the conservation of natural habitat and wildlife. He also owns a farm so we wanted to ask him what changes he had noticed to local flora and fauna during his lifetime both in agriculture and in general.

In his opinion farming had become more of a business than the lifestyle it used to be and global price competition had forced people to be more efficient and cut-throat in the way they manage the land. In his youth, farmers, such as his parents, practised 'mixed farming': a few animals, some barley and a patch of potatoes. There was plenty of marginal land that was left totally untouched. Drainage had to be done by hand, which was a thankless job, so wet areas and water meadows were not farmed while areas of raised bogland were considered useless for agriculture and were left unused. In fact bogs, he argued, were so undervalued that many became dumping grounds for abandoned cars and other rubbish. Thoughts of conservation never entered most people's heads! He remembered meadows with mixed species of weeds, grasses and wild flowers, where mowing and baling was slow and often interrupted by weather, so any sheltering wildlife had the chance to escape. This slow pace he felt, was in direct contrast to what happens today where speed of operation is the norm. Modern ryegrass has replaced the natural meadows. It is grown to produce a dense crop for silage so is smothered in slurry, artificial fertiliser and lime and, when ready, is cut at high speed. Anything in there, especially ground-nesting birds have no chance. Another change he mentioned was that spring sowing of barley used to be the norm and that gave birds the chance to forage on the tilled ground during the winter months. These days, grain is usually sown in autumn and the growing crops kept weed free by applications of herbicides. The weedy margins of years ago were rich in insect life and essential for butterflies, bees and especially birds – like the grey partridge, which was once common in Tyrone, but has long since disappeared. Looking back it seemed to him that nature left alone had the capacity to achieve a balanced state but modern farming methods had distorted the traditional harmony.

I wondered if other species had gone.

'Skylarks, yellow hammers, lapwings, most barn owls, curlews – all absent now,' he confirmed.

'Everyone of a certain age seems to mention the corncrake,' I said.

'Haven't heard one in these parts for sixty years,' he replied dismissively.

'I've seen nothing but rooks and magpies,' I said.

'This is rook country and many long-established rookeries exist in the area. In fact, in the second half of the nineteenth century on the Rash Estate a few miles away, over ten thousand breeding pairs were once recorded. There's a local saying: "When the rooks fly low, rain's on its way. When the rooks fly high, you won't keep dry!"' he said, smiling. 'When I was young we were always about in these lanes and we knew every inch of them. Magpies' nests were often a target and we would clamber up and steal the eggs, but it's rare to see any children out of doors these days. It's as if the Pied Piper has been around and enticed them all away. So the magpies flourish.'

I loved hearing about the countryside as it used to be, so took the opportunity to ask what the other big local changes had been.

'I don't know what the situation is further afield but around here we have lost nearly all the apple orchards, all of the wild flower meadows, many of the smaller woodlands and a good chunk of the raised boglands. Many of the ponds where we used to search for newts have been drained and ploughed and, in recent years, new properties have sprung up everywhere.'

We said goodbye and headed on our way, wondering more than ever whether we'd be able to restore the land to the way it used to be.

Jim was certainly right about the rural building boom: many farmers, eager to draw much-needed capital from unprofitable land, exploited the lax planning laws and sold off potential building sites in their hundreds. Newspapers had pages of planning applications and for a few years farmers, builders and suppliers regarded this unprecedented construction as the new Klondike. Business was brisk, profits were huge and very few people, politicians or members of the general public, seemed to give any consideration to the long-term consequences of this widespread change to the environment. Traditional meadows, bogs and woodlands eaten up by concrete are impossible to replace and few people seemed to have any concern about what was happening to the landscapes. This was a worry to us because we were also about to build a house and therefore contribute to this situation. We promised ourselves that whatever changes we made to the land would ultimately improve it as a habitat rather than despoil it further.

Years after we had acquired the land and begun the wildlife project I took a trip to the local library to examine the historic maps of the area. I discovered to our surprise that we were not the first to have built there. In the 1800s there had been four cottages and many more in the immediate vicinity, showing that the area was once relatively densely populated. In fact, many times during our landscaping we unearthed shaped hearth stones, fragments of pottery and other evidence of previous generations.

Furthermore, the library maps identified three earthworks or tumuli on the tops of the nearby hills showing that the land had been popular thousands of years previously. Perhaps the twenty-first-century building boom was merely replacing the settlement patterns that had existed two hundred, or indeed two thousand, years earlier!

Jim Whiteside's analysis of environmental change and Rosemary's memories of her childhood in the area set us thinking about who is looking after our countryside and preserving what we have for future generations. True, there are organisations across the UK and Ireland working hard to promote conservation and influence national policy and practice, but for much of the landscape it is the agricultural economy that holds sway. Farms in Ireland are generally much smaller than their counterparts in England and for many, especially in the wetter areas, cattle or sheep rearing are the only real options for making a living. Chemical fertilizers and slurry are put on to the land but widespread use of pesticides is not a problem except in the dryer cereal-growing regions. Fewer chemicals there may be but native species of birds, butterflies and wild flowers are still taking a nosedive into oblivion. It would be good to think that the growing awareness of environmental destruction is changing attitudes but certainly in Northern Ireland, a culture of agricultural efficiency over habitat still prevails and is supported by the single farm payment system – annual aerial surveys show where hedges, tree cover or wild habitat are encroaching on the farming acreage, and unless farmers clear the growth and trim the hedges, their payments are reduced. If politicians are really interested in conservation and encouraging the return of wildlife, then surely this kind of criteria should not exist.

At micro level there is one much more positive story: the massive change in attitude towards supporting garden birds across the country. The sale of nuts, seeds and feeding stations has exploded in recent years and gardens are increasingly becoming important as green routes and mini conservation areas. It does seem astonishing that in many places there is now far more wildlife in towns, cities and suburbs than there is in rural areas, a situation that would have been inconceivable a generation ago.

One of the reasons we were attracted to the land we purchased was the view of Seskinore Forest, which is half a mile or so away to the south. This wooded area of a hundred and twenty acres was once an old established country estate. The hall and former grandeur are long gone but the collection of spectacular specimen trees designed to enhance the natural rise and fall of the landscape still exist and show that, given time and effort, this part of the country is capable of supporting a habitat that goes way beyond rushes and wet grasslands. The planting of exotic species at Seskinore – in common with many estates – was not only for aesthetic reasons but was also to enhance the sporting potential of the land. Formal pheasant shoots were popular and the strategically placed copses of oak and beech, old 'snap shooting' rides and sheltered meadows were designed with this in mind.

After the Second World War, when tax demands, increased wages and social change put pressure on these large estates, many became unviable and were split up and sold. Smaller blocks of land then went into private ownership and were cleared for timber or farming and valuable wildlife habitat was lost. We may not agree with the status, exclusivity and privilege enjoyed by earlier landowners, but perhaps we should all be grateful for the legacy of woodlands, planted with sport in mind, that they left behind and that still grace many parts of the countryside today.

The extensive raised bogland on the eastern side of the plot we now owned was an additional attraction. Much of this unique ancient habitat has disappeared across Ireland but we were delighted to discover that, along the boundary of our land, several acres of heather and birch remained largely untouched. There was evidence of old peat-cutting trenches but no workings had been undertaken for many years, and nature had largely hidden the efforts of earlier generations. Luckily the land had escaped the recent building boom – this type of landscape is costly to develop and the ownership of the land is notoriously difficult to establish. In the past, turf-cutting rights were allocated to surrounding farms but the precise boundaries of these areas were often unclear and disputes going back many generations seemed endemic to the local culture. Further confusion arises because turbary (turf-cutting) rights are not the same as land-owning rights. It is largely this lack of clarity that has kept the bogland habitat free from the intrusion of pile-drivers and developers.

Digging for peat had long since been abandoned on our raised bogland because the end product was of poor quality with little calorific value, and because more modern forms of heating have taken its place. Peat is obtained by a process of cutting, drying, carrying, stacking and storing, and its usefulness varies depending on its depth, colour or age. In Ireland the slices of peat are called turves and the fires are turf fires. It surprised me to learn that well into the twentieth century many parts of Ireland kept the peat fires burning the whole year round – banking up the fire at bedtime to keep it safe, and then blowing the embers back to life the next morning.

The culture surrounding 'winning of the turf' still remains strong in the memories of local people. The smell of the peat smoke from a chimney on an autumn evening will instantly bring forth fond tales of days digging, drying or 'clamping' the turf. As a newcomer to Ireland, this romantic view of the practice of peat digging always seemed misplaced to me because it was clearly back-breaking work, utterly frustrating in wet weather and the material from our local bog burned through like newspaper on a bonfire. Whenever I sat next to a peat fire, instead of being able to relax I was constantly up and down fetching further buckets from the shed. I always feel peat warms you three times: once when it is being dug; for a few minutes while it is burning; and again when you are running out with the bucket for another refill.

Having said this, much of the bogland retains an air of wildness and makes an attractive retreat for many kinds of wildlife. The true areas of raised bogland are dry, and cloaked with heather and myrtle, but the old peat-digging trenches flood easily and, given they are covered over with mosses and marsh grass, make the terrain hazardous to negotiate – what appears to be passable, sound land can ambush the unwary. Those in the know advise wearing a flat cap when crossing the bogland because it will stay on the surface as you sink and make it easier for your relatives to find you and get you ready for the wake!

A precise survey of our land identified on the lower sections very wet soils with extensive reed beds, a small stream issuing from the bogland and, in one corner, the banks of what we believed might be the remains of an old flax dam. Rosemary's brother Kevin was eleven years old when his father was killed but he clearly remembered the dam and men working with the flax plants. He confirmed that this part of the farm had always been low-lying, boggy ground so creating a flax dam was seen as the best option. It was an important cash crop for many farmers in the area because the fibres contained in the plant were used to produce linen. After flowering and ripening in July, the flax was pulled by hand and soaked in the small water-filled dams, then left for one to two weeks to 'ret', a process that broke down the tough outer coating. It was spread on the fields to dry and beaten over a stone with a club to separate the fibres or put through a flax mill. It was punishing, unrelenting work where wet hands became permanently sore and no one we spoke to seemed to regret its passing.

Hedges surrounding the property were healthy and contained a traditional mixture of straggly hawthorn, blackthorn, ivy, ash, honeysuckle and dog rose. To our surprise we could find no holly, hazel, beech or yew, but around the site of one of the earlier cottages, crab apple and damson trees formed part of the boundary. The hedgerows crossing the lower wet lands were a very sorry sight and the sodden ground had clearly taken its toll both on them and on the ash trees growing along their length. Tops were dying back and the old hawthorn in many sections would clearly never recover. Clumsy digger work down at one of the ditches had severed the roots of several mature ash trees, effectively killing them. The hillsides were drier but still had a covering of heavy clay, and a pH test revealed a fairly neutral soil.

We found a small, secluded, almost secret natural well on the boundary where an underground spring issued from the hillside. This remained permanently full, even after a spell of dry weather. Rosemary remembered in her early childhood days Old George, an elderly man from a nearby cottage, crossing the field every day to fetch water. At one time I designed a small plaque to fix to the large stone at the side of the well both to commemorate its use in earlier times and to give anyone coming across it a smile. It read:

A man lived for years in the stone cottage at the top of the hill. He crossed the field every day, winter and summer, to fill his bucket and maintained that this 'was the best water in Tyrone'. He died aged forty-two of cholera.

In the end I was persuaded that this might cause offence if George's relatives ever visited – particularly since the man lived well into this eighties and the cholera bit was totally untrue.

The story of George – fondly told – also made me consider again the affectionate way we think about the past. Vintage tractor rallies, All our Yesterdays festivals, replica donkey carts adorning gardens and tales of the 'winning of turf' all promote a nostalgic, romantic view of earlier days that must bear little resemblance to the reality. Eking out a living on these wet unproductive lands was clearly very hard going in the past – no mains electricity, machinery hardly able to cope with heavy soils, often no mains water and few farming subsidies. It is probably true that the romance of poverty disguises the fact that there were few luxuries but at the same time there was a much greater feeling of community. All the neighbours in these rural areas were known to one another and visiting without appointment for a cup of tea and a chat was commonplace. Greater prosperity has certainly brought greater distance and as one elderly neighbour said with some sadness, 'I haven't a clue who lives in any of these houses that have sprung up.' Astonishing how things have changed in one generation!

I don't think either of us realised when we acquired the land just how wet it really was. We always needed wellington boots to get around and there were several parts where concentrations of cattle had churned up the surface and made it totally impassable. In other parts, overgrown ditches blocked the natural flow of water, especially during periods of prolonged rainfall, and the flood poured out on to the fields creating semi-permanent 'swamps'. There are positional and latitudinal limits to what can be done on any piece of land, and we began to worry that ours might turn out to be too wet to become a varied wildlife habitat. In fact, we became so concerned that we sought advice from the local digger man, Lawrence, whom everyone recommended as the expert in draining wet fields. He came round, listened patiently to the plans we had for the place and was instantly practical and positive. He explained that it was not uncommon to find land such as this, which has been rented out for years, abused and neglected but that could soon be put right. Lawrence proposed that, as a start, the ditches would need to be cleaned out and a modern drainage system put in across the centre of the fields, and that we would then see an immediate improvement.

Thankfully his advice was very reassuring.

We have always believed in learning from others but when we searched for other wildlife gardens of similar size in Northern Ireland that roughly equated to what we hoped to do, we failed to locate them or they simply did not exist. Of course there was formal assistance from government agencies and charities about conservation and wildlife but little that was applicable to people such as us who wanted to start from scratch and develop a mid-sized wildlife area. This was frustrating because conservation and the care of our countryside has become a very hot topic in recent years but much of the concern appeared to be academic rather than practical. Finding answers to the many questions we needed to ask was proving difficult. We had acquired the land, with what we felt was a laudable aim in mind, but had no real idea if our hopes for the place were just pipe dreams. The site was much wetter than we first thought, we had seen virtually no wildlife during our close analysis of the land, and we had faced a lot of scepticism about the feasibility of the project from neighbours who knew the area much better than us. We still felt that with energy and optimism we might be able to create something special.

In any case, we now owned the land – the die was cast, so we set out to create the Fod.

'Strange name,' someone once remarked. 'Is it Gaelic?'

Although *fód* is the Irish word for turf, the explanation is much more straightforward. The name just evolved. When our sons rang home, Rosemary would pick up the phone and the conversation would go something like this: 'Where's Pa?'

'He's working at his field of dreams.'

This was eventually shortened to 'he's up at the fod,' and once Bernadette, our daughter-in-law, bought us a nameplate for the entrance, the name stuck.

2

Making a Start

'You're wasting your time,' said the man at the wheel. 'It'll die. I tried it.'

The stranger had stopped his pick-up truck on the narrow lane opposite where we had begun to work and, uninvited, offered his advice.

'I moved some trees last year and they all died. You'd be better making a heap and putting a match to it!'

It was 2003, a cold February morning, crisp and fresh, and the digger had arrived on the low-loader and slowly reversed on to the narrow lane. We were cutting the first entrance into the field when the car stopped. The roadside hedge had no doubt been there for years and was a valuable wildlife habitat of hawthorn, blackthorn, dog rose, ivy and ash, interwoven with a network of honeysuckle and bramble. Disturbing the hedgerow certainly didn't sit easily with us but the planning authorities had strict guidelines about visibility, especially on tiny country lanes, and any new entrance had to have adequate sightlines. This meant ripping out some forty metres of hedge in order to set the entrance to the property back from the road.

'I'll make two heaps over there and we can burn them when they dry a bit,' Lawrence, the digger man, said.

'No, no,' I replied, 'dig a trench five metres in and lift the hedge in sections, taking as much soil and root as you can and replant it all, those small ash trees included. It takes years for a mature hedge like this to develop. Shame to waste it.'

He looked slightly puzzled but set about doing what I had suggested and the digger took a huge bite out of the wet ground.

Modern diggers make short work of tasks that would have taken days only a few years ago – Lawrence had almost finished the transplanting exercise and was firming up the ground alongside the 'new' hedge with the bucket when the man in the car stopped. He repeated his advice that there was no point trying to save the hedge.

'The trees and hedge are dormant at this time of year. If we scoop up enough root and soil there is no reason why it shouldn't take.'

'Tenner says it doesn't,' he said offering his hand out of the truck window.

'You're on,' I said, striding over and shaking hands on the bet. He drove off, shaking his head, still muttering about something.

'Who is he?' I asked Lawrence.

'Lives over by the river. Has advice for the whole world.'

Everybody now calls him Google.

Thankfully the hedge grew well over the next few years and I have stood many times on the roadside hoping to collect the proceeds of the bet. Rumour has it that Google drives several miles out of his way to avoid passing our gate and paying his dues.

This wasn't the only time a driver stopped by our ancient hedge for a chat, but next time it was much more perplexing. It was a warm summer evening and I had decided to shape parts of the foliage that had grown particularly vigorously. The job was finished, the leaves swept up and I was standing back admiring my handiwork when an old green Land Rover stopped. A red-faced man slid back the window and said in a strong Tyrone accent, 'Am I right for a jimmy riddle?'

Well, I didn't know much yet about the locality and its customs but I did know about rhyming slang. Apples and pears, whistle and flute, Mickey Mouse – all of that stuff, and I certainly knew what a jimmy riddle was.

'Help yourself, pal. I've just cut the hedge specially!'

He gave me a strange look, hesitated as if he was about to say something else, shook his head, and suddenly put his foot down and drove off.

'Strange bod,' I said to myself, gathering up my brush and tools.

Later when I was relating the weird encounter to Rosemary, she asked me what exactly he'd said.

'He said, "Am I right for a jimmy riddle?"'

She immediately cracked up laughing and told me that Jim Riddell was our neighbour two farms down the valley.

Gradually we did get to meet people who lived nearby. They do say that in a small country like Northern Ireland you are only ever one person away from someone you know or who is a distant relative. Even in the larger towns, I was struck by how readily strangers will strike up a conversation. They may lead with the weather, but often what they really want to know is more about me. Questions about where I come from and why I am in the area come thick and fast. There is little embarrassment or reserve in the process and some enquiries are very direct, usually during the very first meeting: 'Who are you, then?'

Sometimes the probing is more subtle. At the very start of our project, I visited the local builders' merchant for the first time, part way through a very wet day of digging drains and floundering around in muddy ditches. My appearance could not have been described as immaculate – with my worn old shooting coat, filthy leggings covered in wet clay, wellingtons and battered 'Indiana Jones' hat, I must have been a sorry sight. After I had lodged my order for more concrete pipes, the conversation with the man behind the counter went something like this:

'Where are you building?'

'On land beyond Seskinore Woods.'

'Why did you choose there?'

'I liked the site.'

I had been answering a lot of questions lately, and thought

that I'd try to give away as little as possible. The others in the shop knew the game we were playing and watched the match with interest.

'But you're English – why did you choose Tyrone?'

'Because I like it.'

'It's a big change from living in England.'

'Yes,' I said, 'I suppose it is.'

At that moment my neighbour from the farm further down the valley walked in. He looked wetter and more dishevelled than I was. His coat was in tatters, his boots and leggings bore evidence of the cowshed and his trilby looked like he had slept in it.

'How's it going, Bob?' he asked. 'Bit wet for your kind of work today.'

'Yes. Not the best of times to be digging drains.'

The builder's merchant got in quickly, 'I see you've already met the local villains. How do you know Tom then?'

I looked at my neighbour's bedraggled appearance and replied, 'Oh! We both go to the same tailor.'

Laughter from the onlookers. End of the interrogation. By the next visit, though, he seemed to know as much about me as my mother!

Gaining a negotiable route on to the land was the first problem to overcome. Years of neglect had left it sodden and muddy so getting in with a car was virtually impossible. We had a four-wheel drive Shogun at the time, which also proved useless. Indeed getting through the worst bits was a trial even in wellingtons, and it was very easy to lose a boot in the deeper holes. We needed to make a drive and Lawrence explained what he had in mind. 'I'll cut deep drains at either side of the new roadway, raise the centre up with stones and gradually make the three hundred metres of drive to where you will eventually build your house. For the drive and house we'll probably need sixty to seventy lorry loads of stone from the quarry.'

'That seems a lot,' I said, thinking purely of the likely expense.

He pointed out that water was always going to be a problem on our land, and that it was better to sort it out while the heavy machinery was on site. The open drains he had just excavated had already become mini streams – he went on to explain that he intended to pipe these and cover them over so they ran unseen into an existing ditch.

'One other thing,' he added, and my heart sank a little. 'In my view it would be wise to dig land drains every few metres across these fields taking them down the slope to the lower land in the valley bottom. It will cost you a couple of thousand more – when I have covered them over you won't see anything for your outlay but in the long run it will be money well spent.'

'What does this kind of drainage entail?' I asked.

'I prefer to dig a narrow trench, lay a perforated plastic pipe, fill it up with stone and replace the top soil. You mentioned you might consider creating a lake on that lower land and it would do no harm to make the drains run down into that.'

An existing drainage ditch that brought the surface water down from the neighbouring field crossed the path of the proposed drive and had to be bridged. Lawrence laid substantial concrete pipes, built shuttering around them and poured further concrete in to seal and strengthen the structure. Earlier in the day his digger had unearthed piles of boulders and building stone from the remains of a cottage. There were shaped corner stones, a doorstep and several pieces that looked like windowsills. Bits of broken pottery, an ancient metal hook and a broken cast-iron cooking pot also came to light. 'What tales could these stones tell?' I said to Lawrence, and asked him to make a pile that we could use for the walls of the new bridge. We learned later that the cottage that once stood on this site was the home of Rosemary's great-grandmother, but unfortunately we could find out nothing further about the cottage or indeed the person who lived in it.

The stones recovered from the cottage fitted perfectly on the new bridge and it felt rewarding to be reusing material which no doubt had been very hard won in the first place. Already weathered and worn, these recycled stones made the newly built walls look like they had been there for decades. I also suggested blocking the ditch next to the bridge to create a mini pond, in the hope that the slow-moving water might attract a few frogs at spawning time.

'You mean use the sheugh to form a pond? Would you be happy with that?'

'I probably would be if I knew what a "shuck" was. Is it some kind of German digger?'

He laughed. 'That's a sheugh,' he said, pointing at the water. 'What you'd call a drain or a dyke.'

Well, you live and learn.

Watching an expert driver handle a modern digger is fascinating. The complexity of the controls, the versatility of movement of the arm and bucket, and the speed with which tasks are completed is remarkable. Lawrence's dexterity and coordination with this complicated machine was impressive. Great chunks of wet earth were shifted effortlessly, a thick carpet of stones laid and hammered flat and in no time at all we had a serviceable drive into the heart of the property. We had also built a small bridge and made a tiny pond in the sheugh which we hoped would eventually become a bog garden.

I had spotted a pied wagtail near the new bridge and, knowing that this species likes to nest in walls above water, I had deliberately left a gap in the wall we had built with the old stones. In autumn, after the vegetation had died down, I peered over the low parapet and was delighted to see the remains of a successful nest. Seeing a wagtail in the first place had been exciting enough but knowing our efforts had encouraged the birds to stay and nest was an added bonus. I look back on this as our first wildlife success.

★

One thing we had learnt from our efforts in Nottinghamshire was to look at local gardens to see which plants worked best in particular locations. We had spent ten years experimenting before we arrived at a range of shrubs and plants that thrived on the thin sandstone of Sherwood Forest. We discovered later – to our dismay – that we could have saved ourselves time and expense if we had first visited nearby Newstead Abbey to find out what grew there. The plants in their ancient gardens were almost identical to the selection we had finally arrived at after years of trial and error.

With this lesson in mind I consulted two expert tree and nursery specialists at the Moy in County Armagh, Jim and Andrew Donnelly. In fact our first conversation turned out to be about something much more important – the soil.

'Make sure you disturb only the minimum amount of soil,' Jim said. 'Insist that only the soil around the building is touched and try to restrict the spread of building debris. It takes years for topsoil to settle down once it has been moved, so the less you tamper with it the better.'

We had noticed that most builders seemed to scrape everything off at new sites and leave the soil in a heap at the side during the building process – but Jim told us that this was disastrous for gardens and would stop anything growing for years. We were really grateful for his expert advice.

Our knowledge of garden design was almost nonexistent so we bought gardening books, searched the internet, asked the local experts and realised early on that, although we mainly had the return of wildlife in mind, we would need a basic overall plan to have some degree of cohesion within the whole project. We tried to list the elements that were most important to us – and we now realise that what we finally came up with was fairly standard and traditional:

1. a varied habitat for wildlife
2. plenty of woodland edge (trees bordering open country)

3. ponds or small lakes
4. planting that provides food sources, cover and shelter
5. a wild flower meadow
6. more formal gardens near the house
7. an orchard and soft fruit area
8. a vegetable garden close to the house
9. self sustaining and low maintenance (if possible on this kind of acreage)
10. an outbuilding for equipment storage

We intended to strive towards a wild garden where, in places, nettles, brambles and other 'weeds' could grow unhindered. We would plant up odd corners with native trees and with luck the 'garden' would sit easily in the landscape. In fact, we hoped that as things progressed it would blend in so well that it would be impossible to see where our land ended and the farmland beyond began. We knew there would be no 'perfect finish', no high point as on television makeovers where the garden has to be complete by the end of the programme, because in reality, gardens are always changing and, even with the most optimistic imagination, it was impossible to predict how things would finally work out. Style in a garden is a very personal and subjective thing, and scale also alters every concept, so in an area the size of ours we knew that we wouldn't have been able to maintain a manicured garden even if we'd wanted to. It would have required hours of endless work. A key part of our plan was to create a low-maintenance, self-sustaining plot, if this were possible, that would mature naturally into the attractive wildlife habitat we sought. Urban gardens in the countryside do look misplaced so, although we hoped to radically alter the existing landscape, it was important to us that the finished article would fit comfortably into its country setting.

Television garden-makeover programmes make garden design seem straightforward. Deciding what would work on a five-acre site was, for total amateurs like us, a very daunting task. The most practical solution was not to be overawed by considering the complete site but to imagine it as a series of smaller rooms that we could plan as separate entities and then join together like a jigsaw to see if they created an acceptable master plan. We began by carefully plotting the direction of the prevailing wind, the most sheltered spots, where the sun rose and set, the distribution of wet and dry areas, where frost pockets remained after cold spells and anything else related to the climatic and physical nature of the land. The whole process was one of discovery but in the end we felt we had a reasonable grasp of the way trees, buildings and topography created distinct microclimates, wind tunnels and protected areas.

We measured precise distances across the whole plot using an enormous builder's tape and we drew up the details to scale on large sheets of graph paper. Gradually we began to visualise what might be developed in each block. At that stage I was flying twice weekly to England to run a national scheme for training future school leaders and used the journeys to plan out the different sections. So each week I designed new elements – an orchard, a wildlife pond, woodland blocks, small lakes and formal gardens – before finally bringing all the pieces together to see if the plan worked as a whole. Since we wanted eventually to be able to walk around the whole garden, we tried to make sure there was an unbroken system of paths, steps and green avenues that would link together, and add interest and intrigue. Some of these were straight-line, direct routeways to the garden sheds, greenhouse or vegetable plot; others were planned as meandering pathways through the woodlands or meadows.

We knew there was no single blueprint for making a garden that is attractive to wildlife because different species need different things to thrive. Variety of habitat seemed to be the best answer. Some parts can be neat and tidy; others left rambling and wild. Tree planting will work for some species while others will be attracted to ponds and wetlands. As we had enough space to build this diversity into the habitat and no real idea of what species might exist in the surrounding countryside, we tried to cover all options in our planning.

Now we had a plan, we were itching to get started and especially to plant something. Our first attempt was a disaster but it gave us both a wry smile. I had grown a bay tree in a large container during our time in Nottinghamshire. It stood on a sheltered patio and, since as a family we are very keen cooks, it had been pruned, pampered and used for many years. Each winter it was protected from the frost with a coat of bubble wrap and over the years had grown into a very fine specimen. On the day we moved to Ireland it was hoisted into the furniture lorry, wedged upright with packing and duly transported across to Tyrone. For a while it seemed to suffer no ill effects from the move but after time it appeared stressed. Perhaps, I reasoned, the pot was becoming too small, so I decided to seek out the most sheltered part of the new land and plant it out. With some effort it was loaded on to the trailer, hauled across two very soggy fields by hand and finally planted in what seemed to be a suitable spot. It looked impressive because this was the very first thing that we had planted on the site and we both felt it was truly the start of our dream to transform this land. We walked to the top of the hill, took tea from the flask and returned ten minutes later to find two cows merrily munching the final few leaves of our treasured bay tree!

On a more positive note, I remembered the advice of a talented gardener, who had once advised me that the hedging is key when you are starting a garden from scratch. 'Dividing the plot gives structure and interest and since good hedges are often slow growing, by the time you come to think about your main design, you will already have the bare bones in place.'

Bare-root beech hedging was available and cheap so we decided during March 2003, to separate the upper end of the garden, vegetable plot and orchard from the house with a long dividing hedge. Rosemary and middle son Ed dug the holes and did the planting, and it did seem slightly odd putting in beech when we hadn't even laid the foundations of the house but we reasoned that by the time this was finished the tiny beech slips would already have formed a discernible hedge. On the colder windward side of where the orchard would eventually be we added a parallel hedge with a path in between with the ultimate aim of giving extra protection to the fruit during cold weather. We placed a single wooden gate in the new hedge – since there was not yet anything of note on either side, it looked slightly comical sitting out in the middle of the field.

'The gate to nowhere,' said Lawrence.

'Reminds me of that film *Blazing Saddles*,' said his mate, 'where all the cowboys have to queue up to go through a barrier in the middle of the desert.'

Deciding on the precise style of house we wanted was relatively easy in comparison to deciding about the garden because we had in mind a building that would look like it had been on the site for many years. We were hoping to build a traditional Irish parochial-type house with blue tiles, stone quoins, gravel drive and a half-tower at the front so that we would get a panoramic view of the countryside. At the rear of the house we wanted a courtyard with a covered area against one wall that would give some shelter from strong winds and provide an outside sitting area when days were wet but mild. We viewed dozens of old houses by driving around the countryside and stopping whenever we saw something interesting. I often thought we must have looked a suspicious pair, standing and staring at isolated rural properties, and on a few occasions we felt obliged to explain our actions to their owners. Finally though, we managed to come up with a design that seemed to fit the bill. Lawrence made short work of levelling the site by removing the topsoil where the house would stand but it became instantly obvious why this land was, for centuries, really badly drained. Less than half a metre below the surface was a layer of rock-hard till, impervious and crust-like, and the digger had to work hard to carve out the pattern of the footings that would eventually become our home.

We had put the design out for tender and several local builders responded quickly with their estimates. Early on in the process a young man from the bungalow a quarter of a mile away down the valley turned up. He was Shane, the son of one of Rosemary's cousins, and he asked if he could submit a tender. 'I have a small building company and have built houses previously. Nothing as large as the one you are planning, but that shouldn't be a problem.' Shane was certainly not as experienced as some of the other contractors but we liked his honesty, enthusiasm and the sincere interest he showed in the project so we appointed him builder and site manager.

With Shane and a good team of craftsmen in place we started the building of the house in June 2003. It rapidly began to take shape. Machinery and materials were restricted to the building area and each evening Shane made sure the place was tidied meticulously so there would be minimum disturbance to the surrounding land. I was on site most days and, when possible, Rosemary joined me in the evenings and we had a stroll around the place to check progress. Our dog, Sal, always accompanied us on these visits and though she was very slow, she seemed happy to plod along wherever we went. She was a black Labrador – in her prime she had been very fit and a superb retriever but now, aged sixteen, she was only able to potter round the place at a snail's pace. She slept most of the time but the builders stopping for lunch was her signal to saunter over to see if she could beg a crust or a piece of biscuit. It became a routine. The men would sit round a makeshift table, get out the flasks and sandwiches and begin their daily hand of cards. Sal would be in attendance.

The boss of this particular team never brought lunch and was always cadging a drink, chocolate bar or sandwich from anyone who took pity on him or fell for his excuses. His antics became a standing joke with the men and they ribbed him constantly.

'Can't you afford a flask?'

'Why don't you call in at SuperValu?'

'Is the missus too mean to set you up with a feed?'

It was endless and merciless but seemed to roll off him like water off a duck.

One day he arrived with a brand new sandwich box, banged on the table and in a theatrical manner announced: 'I have here the very best in Tupperware and inside are two of the freshest rolls this side of Belfast. Each one contains two slices of prime beef and the very best butter Ireland produces.' With a flourish he took out one of the rolls and showed it to his audience. 'I am also the proud owner of a new flask which holds four cups of the finest Punjana tea,' he added, and bowed to laughter and a round of applause.

'Do you fancy a hand of cards?' someone asked.

'Why not,' he replied sitting down at the table and putting his new purchases on the floor.

The cards were dealt and the game was getting underway when suddenly the table erupted in laughter that could be heard in the next county. Sal had sneaked in, devoured the first roll and now stood with the second firmly gripped in her jaws. She may have been an old dog but, where food was concerned, whatever she had she was keeping so despite the cries of 'leave', she gobbled down the beef and bread in an instant. It took minutes for the laughter to die down.

Next morning the building team were keen to see if their boss would say anything to me about my dog. Looking deliberately downcast I headed towards the waiting throng.

'Morning, Bob. You all right? You don't look your usual bouncy self.'

'Oh I've been down at the vet's all morning. Dog's not well. Must have been something she ate.'

The dog gave us cause to smile on another occasion that year. A geography teacher at Rosemary's school was ill one day, so I was recruited to take a class to complete river studies in the Sperrins. Sal came along for the ride. Part of the exercise was to measure the flow of water in a mountain stream: one student stood in the water and released the coloured float and others measured its speed until it reached another student downstream. The dog had walked to heel as we left the bus and now sat watching the proceedings with interest. All the students were busy measuring, asking questions, or taking notes and photographs – except for one, who seemed totally uninterested and stood apart from the group with his hands in his pockets, constantly looking over in my direction. I was just about to go over to him to try to get him involved when a shout from the stream made me look up. The 'catcher' at the bottom end of the section of water we were studying had missed the float and it was now racing away into deeper water. Losing it would have been a problem so I told Sal to fetch it.

She had always been a great retriever and a strong swimmer, and she eased herself out into the current and soon overtook the bobbing float as it headed towards the main channel. She came ashore downstream, with the float held gently in her mouth, and plodded back up the bank to deliver her prize proudly into my hand.

'Well done!' I said, patting her head. 'You may be a bit slower than you once were but you've still got it.'

The disengaged student strolled over and said, 'Do you mind if I ask you a question, sir?'

'Of course not – that's what I'm here for,' I replied, happy that he was finally showing interest in his studies.

'That's a great working dog. How much would you take for her?'

What you think you are teaching is often very different from what your students are actually learning!

When the building process was fully underway and the noise of construction was constant, it was sometimes a treat to take time out on the extensive raised bogland area, to the eastern side of the house. Here there were dry heather banks, swampy parts, bog myrtle, mosses and lichen, and it was home only to a few feral goats, some migratory snipe and small colonies of meadow pipits. This land had been untouched for many years, so sitting down in the middle of this empty space on a sunny day was like being alone on a desert island, the breeze making gentle waves across the surface of the heather. It was a place to meditate, recharge the batteries and enjoy the moment. One day, whilst enjoying this place of peace, I saw a small falcon in low, fast pursuit of a meadow pipit. The falcon was acrobatic, constantly changing direction as its prey tried to evade capture, but when it finally caught up with its victim and stopped atop of its prize, I realised the bird I was watching was a merlin. It was a magical moment because up until that time we had no idea that these very rare birds were established and operating on our doorstep.

Later that first autumn this bogland brought another surprise. Lines of men and dogs appeared crossing the land, accompanied by whistles blowing, white flags waving and the sound of gun shots in the distance. A snipe shoot was in progress and, though very few birds seemed to be shot, I did, perhaps for the first time, begin to question whether the commercial, concentrated shooting of these small birds was acceptable or sustainable.

For centuries this tiny bird has been hunted across Europe, initially for food. Though the plucked carcass weighs just a few ounces, records show that in the early 1900s, it was highly valued. Very large numbers were once shot or netted and transported to the cities for sale to support this culinary taste

– at one time snipe must have been very common across wide areas of the British Isles. Its remarkable speed from a standing start and unpredictable take-off made it a suitable sporting challenge so the snipe soon became an essential part of the traditional shooting calendar. Indeed in the late nineteenth and early twentieth centuries snipe shooting became so popular that it was common for wealthy urban gentlemen to rent almost worthless boglands in Scotland or Ireland for the season in order to secure the privilege of hunting the birds. In Ireland, searching the water meadows or bogs for the wintering snipe has for years been a popular pastime; it has always been simply a matter of choosing the right day, getting together a few friends, a couple of good setters and enjoying the outing. The quarry is usually dressed and roasted immediately and served up on toast as an impromptu breakfast.

Interestingly, there has recently been a resurgence of organised driven snipe shooting in Ireland, and parties of shooters from England or Europe regularly visit for this purpose. Unfortunately the number of snipe nesting in the UK and Ireland has unquestionably declined in recent years due largely to loss of habitat. The weird, almost magical, drumming sound made by the two outer tail feathers of the male bird during mating flights is, in many parts of lowland Britain and Ireland, a thing of the past. Some twenty to thirty million snipe still arrive in Western Europe every year from their breeding grounds in Russia, Scandinavia and Iceland but changes in climate and habitat are impacting on these populations and a serious decline is evident.

Although I find the decline of any kind of wildlife alarming, and part of me – in spite of having shot for most of my life – wonders if this bird should be protected, I have little patience with those who move to the countryside and immediately try to change things that have gone on for years – build a new house and then start to complain about the smell of the pig farm next door; get angry when your car is held up for a few minutes while a dairy herd crosses the road; or try to stop all shooting for sport. It may seem a paradox to some that a love of the countryside and all things wild can go hand in glove with hunting and killing for sport, but for many true sportsmen this apparent tension is illusory. Shooting often involves the creation of suitable habitat, care in the choice of agricultural practices, provision of food source and control of some predators, and this can benefit many species alongside those regarded as legitimate quarry. Of course it is in the self-interest of shooting men to plant and preserve woodland, and to set out wild flower meadows and build flight ponds but in so doing they also protect and encourage many other species. Song birds, for instance, flourish in coverts where pheasants are reared because there is a regular food source, especially in the winter months. Crows and magpies are controlled and because of its sporting potential, woodland where shooting takes place is unlikely to fall victim to any kind of urban development. There is still much daylight between the pro-shooting and anti-shooting arguments but, in small, crowded islands such as ours, perhaps coexistence will provide a model that will prove to be the best practical way forward.

Draining the land, building the driveway and the start of the house building had left much of the land looking like a major construction site. On rainy days the exposed earth looked sodden and quite depressing so we were anxious to press ahead with some planting in order to counter this feeling of desolation. We decided to go ahead with planning an orchard and soft fruit area. In Nottinghamshire, on the 'hungry soils' of Bunter Sandstone, the orchard we set out took nearly seventeen years to mature so an immediate start with this part of the project seemed sensible. We put together apple varieties that were recommended as good for growing in our area, and that should give us a long fruiting season. There were early apples through to russets, and a couple of Bramleys as cookers. We decided to try two types of plum and a pear tree for the wall in our planned sheltered courtyard. We also planted raspberries, blackcurrants and gooseberries – enough for us for jams and pies and other culinary delights, and the same again so that there would be plenty left for the birds. When I explained this plan to the nursery owner he gave me a very strange look.

We planted and staked the new trees, their spindly forms in stark contrast to the orchard we had left behind. This had matured magnificently, with branches just touching across the rides. In autumn, fruit was everywhere, and it became one of the absolute joys of gardening there: to be able to sit amongst the trees, listening to birds and bees, and eating a truly ripe apple that had been on the tree a few moments earlier. The taste sensation bears little resemblance to biting into the boring, mass-produced selections that fill up the shelves of our shops and supermarkets, and is something to savour. Looking at the starkness of our newly planted orchard and knowing how many years it would take to mature, the thought occurred to me that it would have been marvellous to lift the old orchard and transport it lock, stock and barrel to this new location. It was the only thing in gardening terms that I truly missed from Nottinghamshire.

Two days after the new fruit trees were in place we arrived at the site to see a shaggy goat with a pair of enormous, curved horns chewing the bark of one of the staked saplings. Though it scuttled off at amazing speed the moment we appeared we knew it would return as it would have already developed a taste for the tender bark.

'You'll need to drive it back to the bogland,' said the builder. 'Use your four-wheel!'

'Who owns it?' I asked.

'No one. It's probably from one of the feral herds that live on the bogland and up on the Fivemiletown Mountains. They can be a pest.'

He went on to explain that all wild goats in Ireland are descendants of semi-domesticated animals that escaped or were deliberately released several hundred years ago. They are not truly wild animals, but because they have survived and multiplied for many generations without any help from humankind, they have developed a wariness and cunning that makes them difficult to control. In many upland parts of Ireland they have become numerous and do real damage to new trees.

I jumped into the jeep and an exciting chase began. The goat could really run and his twists and turns made the chase feel remarkably like an authentic safari hunt. We headed generally towards the bogland but at the last minute the animal changed direction entirely and went back to the public road. It reached the lane and disappeared out of sight in seconds. A round of applause from the builders greeted me when I arrived back at the site but I had barely managed to park the jeep when our site manager Shane's phone started to ring. He lived down the road and his wife had called to say, 'I don't want to worry you but there is a huge goat eating our new hedge.'

More laughter.

Lawrence finally cornered the goat and housed it for a couple of days in one of his sheds. Unfortunately billy goats do stink at certain times of the year so it was loaded up and released to join the feral herd on the Fivemiletown Mountain and that, thankfully, was the last we heard of it!

There is a temptation, when starting a garden from scratch to buy in mature trees to make an instant impact on what may look like a barren construction site but we felt that this probably wouldn't be the right approach for us. The cost of sizeable trees, in pots or root nets, is considerable and we certainly couldn't have afforded enough to make a difference. Immediately after planting they can also be susceptible to being toppled by strong winds, especially when they are situated in very exposed positions. Ireland is great tree-growing country and, in our case, it proved much more effective to plant larger numbers of bare-rooted slips and accept that they would look sparse to begin with. However, we couldn't resist three mature trees. They were expensive and turned out not to be worth the money: the bare-roots quickly caught up with them and, in the end, became much sturdier specimens as they had never been in pots and so made more natural root growth.

During the initial draining and groundwork, the little wildlife that we did see from time to time was disturbed and soon left for quieter locations. We did see rooks, magpies, the occasional blackbird, wrens, robins and a party of jackdaws that occupied the holes in 'Old Jim's Cottage' – a derelict building a few hundred yards away. Though we believed in the aspiration that *if you build the right habitat, wildlife will come,* that hope has to go hand in hand with reality. Ultimately, the range of wildlife we would be likely to attract was dependent on what existed in the broader neighbourhood. If there were species we had not yet spotted, such as barn owls, jays, finches or tits, then we had a chance. If these were totally absent, no amount of habitat enhancement was likely to succeed. Put another way, if the nearest skylark population was sixty or so miles away in Donegal these lovely birds were never going to find us whatever we did! Our new mantra, which was a bit more long-winded than the original but perhaps more realistic, became: *If we build the right habitat and if they are in the area and like what they find, then maybe they will stay.* Our dream was that as newcomers to the area, we had misread what the local countryside had to offer. Perhaps hidden amongst the hedgerows, woodlands and boglands were flora and fauna that would one day surprise us.

It happened sooner than either of us had expected. One morning, a few months after we had started out, I was standing in the newly created sheugh, checking to see if the water was draining through the system properly, when I saw a female sparrowhawk darting at high speed down the line of the drain towards me. She treated me like any other natural obstacle and lifted up from ground level at the last second, flicked over my shoulder so close to my face that I felt the wind of her passing, then twisted up and over the hawthorn hedge and was gone. Magnificent!

3

Water

Work on the site continued throughout the summer of 2003. Ireland is often associated with constant rain but during July and August of that year blue skies prevailed. The days were deliciously warm and the surface of the land began to dry up. Although the recently installed land drains had made an impact, at this stage it was still hard to imagine that we would ever create the kind of habitat we had in mind. Heavy machinery had made a mess of much of the surface – the disturbed land looked unappealing to us and definitely held nothing to attract any local wildlife. On many mornings during that period, in spite of the beautiful weather, we looked out at the desolation and wondered whether we were right in the head to set out on this kind of enterprise. Then pure chance intervened to revive our flagging spirits and restore our faith.

On the northern boundary of the site, straggly hawthorn and blackthorn hedges converged to create an arrowhead of enclosed land that was overgrown and remained very swampy. We had followed the shape of the land and aimed the pipes – which would drain the new orchard – down the slope towards this wet area. As yet we were undecided about what to do with this neglected corner but as it turned out, events we had not anticipated guided our hands. The dumper trucks we had been using to cart the stones on to the drive were parked overnight and, when we returned in the morning, they had sunk up to their axels in the soft ground.

'Hard to see what we can do with this bit,' said Lawrence after we had hauled the machines out of the mire. 'Our new drains will make this worse, especially in the winter.' We both puzzled for a while and then I had an idea. 'Scoop the whole lot out and make a small pond. Aim at something about ten metres by five and use the excavated material you remove to make a path down the left-hand side. Leave a tiny island in the middle and then we'll just see what nature makes of it.'

A few hours later this impromptu plan was put into action. Though the place was now an ugly construction site, the new pond filled up at an impressive rate and we thought that in a few years it might have potential as a wildlife corner. However this end of the plot was exposed to the westerly gales, which can be remarkably strong at times, and it was obvious that we would have to plant some kind of shelter belt to make the pond appealing. We needed something quick-growing that could survive the wet ground. In the end we were persuaded by a friend who lived a few miles away to try bamboo as a windbreak. He had extensive patches of the plant on his farm and offered us as much as we needed. Freeing up the roots of this established bamboo was no easy task – we needed a felling axe to chop through the matted base – but eventually we had gathered up enough to create a planting. Rosemary totally disapproves of bamboo and feels it is an alien species that spreads alarmingly, a little like laurel and rhododendron, which in many parts of the country have got out of hand and now dominate much of the natural vegetation. To me, the plant has merits. The landscape in Tyrone can look slightly colourless and drab in winter once the leaves have fallen, and evergreen bamboo does provide variety. The plant soaks up water in very wet spots and, even on the stillest of days, the leaves create a relaxing, soothing rustle. It is true that, though the plant can be quite difficult to establish initially, it has to be kept under control, especially in small gardens. However, we had spaces we needed to fill, and I was happy to see it expand. Rosemary remains unconvinced!

At one point in those first few months I planted a row of peas in what would eventually become the vegetable garden to see just what, if anything, the soil might produce. The disturbed land was wet and contained some subsoil so, predictably, the peas failed miserably. However the supporting willow sticks I had cut from the hedge grew and I planted the largest of these at the edge of the new pond. Milder winters and the moist climate mean Ireland is superb for growing trees and in a very short time the pea stick was a super tree with a girth a foot wide.

It reminded me of an odd conversation I once had with a stranger who was walking by and saw me planting a rowan tree. He stopped and said sourly, 'There is an old saying in these parts that a man who plants a tree never lives to sit under it.'

'A man who never plants a tree doesn't understand what a privilege it is to sit under a mature one,' I replied.

'What?' he said.

'Nothing,' I answered, not wishing to waste any time on a pointless lecture about the rate of tree growth in this part of the world. Thankfully, the willow was just the first of many trees to grow well on our site, and after ten years many of the tiny whips we eventually planted were almost large enough to hold a tree house and certainly big enough to sit under!

I can't claim that we planned it this way, but our small pond with its tiny island had turned a neglected swampy area into a secluded haven. It was surrounded with old hawthorn and blackthorn hedges, threaded through with scented honeysuckle and dog rose, and was protected from the wind by the newly planted bamboo. It was instantly a secret place, private and comforting, and the addition of our first garden bench on the sunny side made it a grand place to take the weight off, relax and let the world go by. Gardens need havens for contemplation, and sitting there in the sun with no sound of human activity is a joy which has never diminished. This corner restored us and renewed our optimism in the project.

Of course the banks of the new pond still looked bare of

vegetation so we rushed to the gardening books to choose the most suitable waterside planting in the hope of improving the look of the area. We need not have bothered. Within weeks native plants – such as yellow iris, mare's tail, pondweed and reed mace – had miraculously appeared and were beginning to cloak the margins and give the pond a permanence, as if it had been there for years. These native plants must have been part of the swampy area before the digger disturbed them, split their roots and unknowingly replanted them as the various banks were constructed. That's the logical explanation – but the speed of their appearance seemed almost magical, as if they had been waiting for us to come along and awaken them.

Just a few weeks later I was sitting by the pond, admiring the now-clear water and the strong sunlight illuminating the underwater world when I saw movement. A smooth newt swam into view. It was well marked and attractive, with an orange belly and conspicuous spots, and to my absolute delight he was accompanied by at least twenty others. I knew these tiny creatures were widespread in Ireland, hibernating in winter under logs or in holes, but had no idea they were around our plot and certainly not in such numbers. Newts have become scarce in many parts of the UK, as water tables shrink or ponds are drained, so it was wonderful to discover that we had a thriving colony. We had no idea how they had managed to congregate so quickly in our new pond but were grateful that they seemed to find the new habitat to their liking.

Frogs, water beetles and a host of other aquatic insects also took up residence. One morning when we arrived at the pond a grey heron stood motionless by the water's edge waiting for any unwary frog. It squawked at our approach and then lumbered into the air, legs dangling like a pterodactyl. Later that summer we noticed something had changed slightly on the tiny island. The base of the grass seemed denser, browner than before – the binoculars revealed a mallard duck sitting on eggs. So, in two short months, we had encouraged native plants, and managed to attract newts, frogs, beetles, a heron and a mallard, all in one tiny corner of the garden. It was, to say the least, an encouraging start.

The arrival of a mallard was perhaps the least surprising event: in late evenings we had often seen parties of teal and mallard, high in the sky, moving between their favourite feeding grounds. Much of Northern Ireland is wet country and duck are usually plentiful, but the main populations tend to be more numerous on the main river systems, the Fermanagh Lakeland area and the coastal marshes. Inland, there are fewer, but our hope was that the many small streams and rivers nearby could hold resident populations that we might eventually attract by the creation of additional lakes at the foot of the valley.

Choosing the right place for this venture was not difficult. There was a naturally swampy corner – the site of the old flax dam – that was also the place to which our newly laid drains took water, and where the overflow from a small nearby stream lay after periods of heavy rainfall. Running water is essential to keep ponds from becoming stagnant and in this we were lucky because the bogland spring continued to run even in the driest periods. In fact, Irish raised boglands act like giant sponges, soaking up enormous quantities of water during heavy rainfall, so the springs and streams leaving them never run dry. Though the water is often stained slightly brown by the peat, it is uncontaminated, well oxygenated and is unlikely to freeze in the winter. This wet, neglected corner seemed an ideal place for our new lakes.

Our plan was to dig two lakes, joined in the centre by a feeder channel. They would both be sizeable, with one set at a slightly lower level so that there would be a continuous flow of water through the system. Water supply would come in from the bogland stream at the top end of the system, flow through into the lower lake and then return to the original watercourse at the bottom end. Any very heavy rainfall would bypass the lake system and drain away along the existing course of the stream, which we felt should be left untouched. In this part of Ireland prolonged and heavy rainfall can turn tiny streams into raging torrents in hours and it was vital that these unpredictable surges had an outlet rather than pouring directly into the new lakes to cause flooding or damage.

We managed to obtain consent and some guidance from the various authorities. Lawrence returned with his digger, we rented two dumper trucks, and in early summer 2003 the project began. Lawrence took levels using a rented laser machine and drove in marker poles across the whole site to establish exactly how much ground we would need to remove. Since wildfowl love margins, we incorporated protruding spits of land and bays into our design, as well as a central island. During the breeding season drakes patrol the area they can see, so one simple oval lake will only support one pair of duck. Put in enclosed bays, small islands and promontories and many more breeding pairs can be accommodated. We also intended to create shallow feeding areas for the dabbling wildfowl with deeper parts for the diving ducks. The channel between the two new ponds would be lined with concrete to prevent erosion during the winter rains but we hoped that boulders set into the wet mix would give the impression that this protection was natural rather than artificial.

One major consideration when excavating ponds of this size was what to do with the earth that is removed – it is astonishing how much earth comes out of a sizeable hole. We had two plans. We would use some earth to build up a raised bank on the boundary, to give an elevated walkway around the water and to help to keep the land secure from cattle or sheep. We would transport the bulk of the material up the hill and place it on either side of the drive near the entrance to the property. This would raise the level of the land and leave the feeling that the driveway was running through a 'mini valley'. We hoped that once trees were established on both banks and touched over the roadway visitors would have the experience of driving through a shady green tunnel before emerging into the daylight and the view of the garden beyond.

Having set the levels and marked out the boundaries of the two new ponds, we started to dig. As before, Lawrence made it look easy, and in no time a substantial hole began to materialise. He lifted great scoops of reed bed, matted grass and wet earth and placed them into the two nine-ton dumper trucks – the long arm of the digger reached out, sliced into the earth and almost filled the dumper in one easy motion. Lawrence gave instructions about where each load should be tipped depending on its composition: soil that we might reasonably be able to use in the garden went to one section, hard till to another and the heavy blue clay to a third.

I drove one dumper truck and a colleague of Lawrence's drove the other. Suspension on dumper trucks is designed to go over very rough terrain – each wheel seems to act independently of the others in order to negotiate uneven holes and ridges. Driving one is a strange sensation in rough country as the driver is shaken up and down and from side to side, an experience that can be very tiring on the back.

The other driver summed it up: 'Spend a day on these things in this kind of country and you'll need a hot Radox bath before tomorrow.'

With me it was different. I'd had backache on and off since my rugby-playing days and I fully expected that spending eight hours being thrown around on the dumper seat would prove troublesome. Amazingly the opposite occurred. All the vertebrae seemed to be shaken into line and my back problems virtually disappeared from that day onwards. Perhaps a day on a dumper should be prescribed in back therapy!

Our aim was to make the larger pond six feet deep on average but, in three places, we dug much deeper holes of twice that depth to ensure that if we ever introduced fish there would be deep sections that would never freeze. The second pond would be three to four feet deep and, with several small islands, would hopefully be ideal for duck and other waterfowl.

Making these artificial ponds ran the risk of failure – and many locals clearly thought it a hare-brained scheme that was doomed from the start:

'Built ponds in this country always leak or become stagnant.'

'Digger and liners will cost a small fortune.'

We did wonder whether or not the underlying subsoil would hold water and if the spring water would flow through the whole system as we hoped.

Lawrence always had confidence in the project and quite rightly predicted that we were unlikely to need any kind of liner in the ponds to contain the water because most local land is underpinned by very hard till or, in the valley bottoms, impervious blue clay. Once he got deep enough, he hammered down hard with the bucket – the blue clay hardened like concrete and became totally watertight.

In three days the main excavation was completed. The stream from the bogland was diverted and almost immediately the new pond began to fill. Nothing leaked and it was very satisfying to visit each day and see the water level creeping up towards the point where it would begin to flow over into the lower lake. When the moment finally came I stood with Rosemary and some of the builders by the joining channel to watch the outcome. First a tiny trickle, then a steady flow followed by a cheer from the onlookers as we knew instantly and with some relief that the design was right. Without doubt the ponds would maintain a constant level, would be continuously replenished with fresh water and, because they had a natural outlet, would not flood after periods of heavy rain. Our two ponds were completed by autumn 2003. Once they were finished, and the water cleared and rose to the planned level, we knew instantly that this new habitat would be a magnet for many kinds of wildlife.

The downside was that in order to excavate the ponds, lay the drainage pipes, transport the surplus earth and build the walkways around the margins, we had caused major disturbance to the existing landscape. Although we were very pleased with the finished product the whole area did look like a very raw construction site. On the windward side the water was exposed and, when there was any kind of wind, waves would form, making the site cold and unattractive for wildfowl. We needed to plant some shelter belts!

Buying land and building a house and drive do not come cheap so we had to think of the wildlife garden as a long-term project and do any planting in the cheapest way possible. It is always irritating how the cost of the design is seldom taken into consideration on garden-makeover shows. As every amateur gardener knows, buying mature shrubs, established pot-grown trees or sizeable plants can be hugely expensive. Most of us have to buy small and let time develop the design. Given the acreage we had and the sheer number of plants we would ultimately need, there was no choice but to look for the cheapest option.

In this we got lucky. A local garden centre was changing its emphasis from general plant supply to the public, to growing and distributing specialist products to the wholesale market. Before he'd changed tack, the owner had ordered a large number of bare-root trees for the winter season. These were in bundles of fifty whips and were set temporarily in a bank of moist peat. He explained that they were mixtures of alder, rowan, birch and three types of willow, as well as a few mixed bundles, and that we could have them at rock bottom price. The deal was done. We loaded five hundred assorted trees into the trailer but before I left the owner came up to the car.

'I like what you are trying to do over at your place – there should be more of it,' he said. 'I've got half a dozen Austrian pines and a couple of laurels you can have. No charge. They will give you a bit of greenery during the winter months.'

Our wildlife project was beginning to get noticed.

We planted the alders and willows around the new lakes – and began to feel as though we were finally making some progress. The mixed trees were placed either side of the drive where the surplus blue clay had been dumped – we had severe reservations about their chances of survival because the disturbed soil looked heavy, poorly drained and rocky. In the event our fears were groundless because once the trees hit the nutrients that were contained in this lakeland clay they made better growth than any others on the site. We deliberately planted the whips quite close together so that we would have some instant cover but we knew that we would have to take out alternate trees as they matured.

Native plants began to appear in the lakes almost immediately, just as they had in our first smaller pond. Within weeks the new ponds began to green up around the edges and to look a lot less barren, especially once the water finally cleared. Before the end of the first season, the margins of the ponds were well cloaked with reed beds, iris and floating pondweed. Even in the early days, newcomers often assumed that these wet areas were natural rather than freshly built, which was highly satisfying.

A bit later that same autumn, I was watching the water flow gently along the channel between the two lakes when I noticed minnows shooting about in the current. We had no idea that the bogland stream supported any kind of fish but seeing them there tempted us to introduce a few larger fish to see if they too would survive. We gained permission to put some rainbow trout into the new ponds – we then purchased some, carted them over to the lakes in two tubs filled with iced water and unceremoniously tipped them in. We hoped they might attract herons, or possibly otters if there were any in the area, but perhaps the real reason was that as a lifelong angler, I just love to sit at the water's edge and watch a good trout rise to a fly! The fish thrived and natural food must have been abundant because in two years the trout seemed to double in weight and since then some of them have

The land had been neglected for many years.

Parts were almost impassable.

We often wondered what we had taken on!

Imagination was essential when the machines moved in.

Huge satisfaction at seeing a plan come together.

Fourteen years of hard work was certainly worth the effort.

Boatswain considers the construction of the new lake.

And a few years later Joe takes full advantage of the changed landscape.

Izzy supervises work in the garden.

The pure pleasure of growing vegetables!

More formal gardens can attract wildlife …

… as can typical Irish meadows with their knapweed and meadowsweet.

Joe and his uncle Matt show that gardens can be places of excitement as well as havens of peace and tranquillity.

grown into very substantial fish. With hindsight, I realise that it was certainly not advisable to introduce fish until the water had completely settled down and the normal ecological cycle had become well established. In this respect we were lucky that the fish survived. Purists argue that only native brown trout should be used in these kinds of enclosed ponds but they are more difficult to obtain and rainbow trout do put on weight at a faster rate – though they will never breed so repeat stockings will be necessary. I was interested to know just how long rainbow trout live in the sort of water we had and I was given estimates of between three and five years by the experts with the caveat that we were likely to lose some fish to natural predation. Without doubt some fish from that very first stocking still survive in the deepest holes and, eight years on, it came as a complete surprise to see a trout that must have weighed well over three pounds roll on the surface to take a fly. Though it looked darker than normal, perhaps because of the peaty water, it seemed to be in perfect condition. When I am down by the water, I always keep my eyes peeled in the hope of spotting this fine fish again.

Visiting these newly created lakes became a daily exercise and sitting by the water never disappointed. There was always something fresh to observe – but we soon understood that the changeable weather in this part of Ireland meant that some kind of shelter on the edge of the new pond would be useful. There was plenty of surplus timber from the construction of the house so our son Matt used this to build a hut. With the application of a few coats of green paint, camouflage nets and a bench made from old Land Rover seats we had a makeshift wildlife observation hide.

At this stage in my professional career, I had been asked by the UK government to run a training programme for future school leaders. The two- or three-day courses were generally held in London so at the end of the sessions I joined the crush on the Underground, battled through the security lines at

Heathrow and caught the evening flight back to Belfast. Though I thoroughly enjoyed the work and loved London, it was always a great pleasure to come back to Ireland, to taste the clean air and appreciate the empty motorway on the way home to Omagh.

Sometimes, especially if I had been away for any length of time, I called in at the site on my way home to see what progress had been made in my absence. One still evening just before it got dark, I was sitting, still in my pinstripe suit, in the observation hut next to the water. It was totally relaxing, and a place of peace and tranquillity after my work and journey. I was just thinking how privileged wealthy people were who could afford a flat in London and a country retreat when a strange sound disturbed me. It came from a nearby tree – it was like the movement of a creaking gate or a rusty hinge and was repeated every few minutes. For a moment I thought one of the builders was still on site but then realised it was coming from the ivy at the centre of an ancient ash tree. I had absolutely no idea what it was until an owl appeared out of the gloom and flapped up towards the source of the sound.

'Long-eared owl and chick,' I said aloud, amazed that something I had only read about was there in front of me. The day in London was instantly forgotten.

The original plans for the house and garden that we had submitted to the planning authorities outlined our intention of building pillars at the entrance to hold a pair of wrought-iron gates, to be supported on either side by a six-foot-high wall. This was thought necessary because at the top of the ridge the westerly winter winds came in at pace during stormy weather and the wall would give some protection to the new trees. We planned to plant up the leeward side of the wall with native trees, and to encourage ivy along the exposed windward face, with the hope that in a few years the whole construction would green

over and blend into the landscape. We had noticed during the time we toured the countryside looking at house designs, that many of the older properties had identical coping stones on their main entrance pillars. These were clearly the standard design two hundred years ago and we felt it would be good to link with local historic tradition and replicate this old style on our gates.

One day I was planting some additional ivy cuttings on the roadside wall when the local planning officer arrived.

'We have received a complaint that you are in breach of planning regulations.'

'In what way? We submitted full plans and your office approved them. What exactly is the problem?'

'We have received a complaint that your boundary walls here are too high and we are obliged to follow up all objections to planning decisions.'

'Too high? I don't understand.'

'Boundary walls can be up to six feet high without additional planning but apparently yours are six feet two inches.'

'Have you measured them?' I asked incredulously.

'Me personally, no. In fact I think the walls and entrance blend in perfectly with the countryside – exactly what we try to encourage.'

'Then what is the problem?'

'Regulation. The person making the complaint obviously knows the rules about boundary walls, has measured yours and has submitted the complaint so unfortunately I have to follow it up.'

'Are you at liberty to give me the name of the complainant?'

'Afraid not, but you will probably guess who it is since he is familiar with planning regulations.'

I had a good idea who was responsible.

'It's trivial,' the officer went on. 'In my view your entrance and walls are excellent, especially with the ivy, and if you submit a new application for the height of the walls I will push it through quickly. Unofficially, you might like to know that in the office we have a special folder for this kind of complaint – we call it the "Sad Git File".'

Remaining within the law cost £220. One hundred and ten pounds an inch. It is difficult to understand why someone would go to the bother of measuring a country wall that harms no one then submit an objection merely to cause trouble but 'there's nowt so queer as folk', as the old saying goes.

Early on in our project, we found that we needed more space to house garden tools, mowers, strimmers and all of the general paraphernalia associated with country living. For a patch the size of ours we needed to buy the best labour-saving devices we could afford: we ended up with a ride-on mower, a large push strimmer for the longer grass, a petrol hedge cutter and a power saw. These all needed to be stored so I consulted Niall, who is a first-rate bricklayer and the brother of Shane the contractor, and asked him to build us a shed on land that was shaded by mature ash trees and so would be of little use for any kind of planting. We felt it had to blend in so asked if he could build it old style: 'Small windows, roughly plastered walls, tin roof, rough doors. Make it look as if it has always been there.'

He looked a little doubtful because his work in the area was known for its quality and meticulously high standard.

'I'll try,' he said.

The shed quickly took shape and though Niall clearly hated plastering the walls with wavy patterns, by the time it was whitewashed it did look as if it had been there for a least half a century.

'Perfect job, Niall! All we need now to complete the picture is a donkey looking out over the door.'

In an odd way, we came close to getting one. It went like this. Our local shop was run by a man, nicknamed Jovial Jim – he knew all the gossip but saw misery in everything. He gathered and distributed all the local news to his customers, with particular emphasis on anything which smacked of doom or gloom. One Sunday morning I went to get a paper.

'Morning, Jim! You look a bit fed up,' I said.

'You'll never guess what's happened now,' he said with a face so glum that I feared some real catastrophe had befallen him or the world. A sudden bereavement? Deadly terrorist attack? Major accident? Had we invaded somewhere else?

'What's happened?' I asked with genuine concern.

'Last night some bugger burnt the donkey's arse!'

'Whose donkey? Was it killed?'

'No. Not a real donkey, the plastic donkey on the green.'

Earlier in the year, the local council, in order to brighten up a drab part of the main street, had thought it appropriate to put a larger-than-life plastic donkey and geranium-filled cart on the grass verge at a fork in the road. It looked decidedly tacky, would have looked more at home on a fairground and did little to enhance the village. Though I hated vandalism of any kind, I knew it was going to be hard for me to mourn its passing.

'Where is the donkey now?' I asked, trying to stifle a smile.

'The council took it away.'

'Where to? The burns unit?'

'No the council tip,' Jim said, without showing a vestige of humour.

Some fell on stony ground, I thought.

'I'm sure they'll patch him up and he'll soon be back in harness,' I said paying for my morning paper.

'I don't think so,' said Jim, 'half his arse is gone. He'll not recover from this. He'll be buried at the tip.'

Jim loved any excuse to feel outraged or offended and somehow the plastic monstrosity had metamorphosed inside his head into a real animal.

'Disgraceful,' I said as I left the shop and under my breath, 'I think I'll give the USPCA a ring.'

Driving home the notion came to me that the demise of the village donkey could be a blessing in disguise – just the thing I had been looking for to complete my old-style shed. He could look out over the stable door, would be cheap to keep, would need no mucking out and it wouldn't matter a jot that he was only half the donkey he used to be. The response from the council to my call was definitely lukewarm. No one seemed to know or care where the 'remains' had gone. So, after repeated calls, I reluctantly gave up the chase.

Some weeks later a white-van-driver friend of mine spotted the donkey at another council tip. Someone had placed him looking out over a hawthorn hedge that ran alongside the main road.

'Hey! There's that plastic donkey with the burnt arse. My mate's been looking everywhere for him,' he said stopping the van.

'He wants a plastic donkey with a scorched arse? He must be one sad boy,' said his workmate, not taking his eyes off the tabloid he was reading. 'Drive on.'

After Lawrence had completed his work with the digger on the section of the land next to the new lakes – the land that we hoped would one day become a wild flower meadow – it was necessary to level it off. The family own a Ferguson tractor, which Rosemary's brother Kevin keeps in perfect working order, and with a two-blade plough we began to work the field. Experts make ploughing look easy – leaving the fields like pictures in story books with shiny furrows all ramrod straight, no grass or vegetation sticking out, and neat and orderly turns at the end of each run. The whole exercise appears simple and straightforward. My effort wasn't like that! The rows wobbled along, turns were ragged and the depth of the furrow varied. Sometimes grass and other vegetation stuck out at odd angles where the turning earth had not quite buried it – all in all it looked a pretty amateurish job. It did get better with practice and towards the end I was beginning to feel quite proud of my efforts. A proper tractor man came up to rotivate the field after I had completed the task.

'What do you think of the quality of the ploughing?' I said, 'Not bad for a beginner, eh?'

He said nothing for a minute then muttered dismissively, 'Won't make a deal of difference either way once I've gone over it with the power harrow.'

Which I took to mean he thought the ploughing was rubbish!

I was asked by one local farmer who was considering building a lake about the overall cost of the project.

'For the hire of the digger and the bare root trees, about twelve hundred pounds,' I said.

'That's a lot,' he replied, pulling a sour face.

'To lovers of wildlife and the countryside, the pleasure we get from a walk around it each morning is already worth at least fifty pounds a day and as it matures the value will increase, so twelve hundred pounds seems a real bargain.'

I am not sure he understood or agreed.

4

The Wild Garden

The new lakes had proved a great encouragement both to us and to the local wildlife, but there was still a long way to go. How on earth should we begin to plan and plant for wildlife? There are lots of recommendations out there, but even we knew that what is good for one species can be detrimental to another. It was all pretty confusing for the first-time conservationist.

The trouble was neither of us was a wildlife 'expert' – we had virtually no knowledge of biodiversity or the thousands of flies, bugs, beetles and spiders necessary to support a balanced food chain. We were thinking only of birds and had little understanding of what needed to be done to create an area attractive to *all* wildlife. It took us some time to realise that we were focusing on the popular species, the African elephants or Bengal Tigers of the UK, but that they are only the visible tip of an essential pyramid. Below them are thousands of less glamorous insects and invertebrates vital to a healthy food chain but largely unidentifiable to us. Our understanding of garden design and suitable planting schemes was also scant but we felt our energy, optimism and ability to learn would eventually overcome these shortcomings. We had a dream of how the land could look in the future, and we imagined the wildlife recognising our efforts and coming from all corners to enjoy it. Our naive confidence was challenged on many occasions but we just soldiered on.

We joined the local gardening club and enjoyed meeting the members and learning from them – but unfortunately no one had any particular experience of wildlife gardening on a large site. What works for normal-sized gardens doesn't scale up to meet the needs of several acres.

Visiting all of the notable gardens in Tyrone and surrounding counties for ideas and inspiration, though enjoyable, was at times frustrating and unhelpful. Some of the gardens were magnificent – wonderful places with stunning vistas and a range of trees and shrubs most gardeners can only dream of – but they all had the advantage of age. There were beautiful trees – cedars of Lebanon, oaks, yew and beech – that had been there for a couple of hundred years and gave the kind of structure and grandeur to these places that our bare patch would never have in our lifetimes.

Interestingly, some of the gardens we visited, although they had mature trees, had not been designed for conservation and held little attraction for the wide spectrum of wildlife we hoped to encourage. What was a revelation to us was the way the herbaceous borders in some of these spectacular gardens attracted butterflies, bees and clouds of other insects. We always assumed, wrongly as it turned out, that wildlife gardens have to be stereotypically wild, with abundant brambles and nettles, for example, but this was clearly not the case. There is a perception that an abandoned garden where nature has taken over is best for wildlife, so it was reassuring for us to see the evidence that a traditional garden with well-kept herbaceous borders was not off-putting for the kinds of creatures we wanted to attract. All our research led us back to the philosophy of taking a chance and hoping for the best – we tried to imagine how the future landscape might look and the best ways to plant to attract the wildlife we were so keen to see re-established.

The cost of setting out our future garden was also a significant factor in our plans. It was clear that the building of the house was going to exceed our initial estimates – floor tiles, shower rooms and the kitchen proved much more expensive than we had anticipated. The maxim 'you get what you pay for' is as true as it has ever been and we reasoned we were only going to build the house once and we might as well go for top-of-the-range materials and fittings rather than skimp on quality. As Rosemary often reminded me, unfortunately we both have champagne taste but beer money!

The house building was proceeding as planned and our young site manager was proving to be an inspired choice. He had planned the process meticulously: as each team finished their work, the next was available and ready to start. The builders had laid the first block in June 2003 and by Christmas it was beginning to look like a real house. Though we felt the traditional design was exactly right and would eventually sit really well in this rural setting, to begin with it did look stark and obtrusive. Lawrence had terraced the slopes down to the ponds so the water could be seen from all of the rooms at the front of the house but this too had left the landscape earthy and bare. The round tower with its panoramic view of the countryside was a real winner – if our wildlife project worked, the upper storey would make the perfect vantage point.

It seemed sensible to concentrate our early planting efforts away from the house – building was going ahead at a pace and gardening or tree planting there would be totally impractical and a nuisance for the craftsmen. Jim and Andrew Donnelly from the nursery in the Moy advised us to start by thickening up the boundaries and existing hedges using bare-root whips that were cheaper and did not need staking, and to fill up any odd corner with a mixture of larch, rowan, oaks, ash, wild cherry and hazel. They recommended alder and willow on the wetter land, and planting closely so that we did not have to wait years before it looked like anything – with the plan that we would remove some of the trees at a later date if necessary. Some other good advice was to use the odd pine for greenery, and to plant up the edges with red and yellow dogwood because the landscape can look a bit drab and colourless in this part of the world in winter. And to thicken up the existing hedges they thought holly, yew, hazel and *Rosa rugosa* would work best, with additional hawthorn to hold it all together.

We set out with enthusiasm to follow their suggested blueprint, and found the physical act of planting the tiny trees was straightforward, speedy and highly satisfying. Unfortunately we quickly discovered that in some parts of the land, the holes we dug often filled with water, despite the fact that Lawrence had put land drains across the whole site. Few trees of the type we were planting would survive sitting in water so we reverted to building up mounds of soil and placing the trees above ground level, which seemed to work. I always thought laurel, for instance, would thrive anywhere but one short hedge we had planted, to form a boundary to the 'formal' garden we hoped to create, was soon very unhappy and yellowing. The roots were sodden and the plants would certainly have died entirely had we not dug them out, built up a ridge of soil and compost and replanted at a higher level. This worked and was a planting technique we used thereafter.

Easy work it may have been, but planting any kind of tree is something special. It is a landscape legacy; something that will exist for many years after we have gone, if done correctly, and will become a marker of our efforts. It is a sobering thought that whatever we do in life – however successful or notorious we have been – will almost always have been completely forgotten within two generations, even by our own families. It will be as if we never existed. But plant a tree, or put in a new spinney or woodland and something of us will exist for generations. A few miles away from our house there is an avenue of ash trees, planted both sides of a narrow lane so that they form a spectacular canopy, and I always wonder who put them there. They are not near a house or farm and do not form part of an old country estate so there seems to be no specific reason why anyone should have gone to the trouble of creating this beautiful avenue – but someone did. It is a very satisfying thought that in another hundred years someone might be asking similar questions about our planting. Trees we plant will be around for a long time – that is why the job needs to be done very carefully.

I once watched a landscape architect spend the best part of a day planting a red oak in his garden. He placed the tree and container on the lawn, circled it, took photographs from every angle and repeated the process ad infinitum. It was only when he was satisfied that it was in exactly the right place that he planted it.

'Are you so careful with every tree you plant?' I asked.

'Mistakes will irritate for ever. It is worth taking time to imagine future growth, how the tree will eventually be affected by sun or shade and how it relates to the other plants. Get it right and every year brings added joy. Get it wrong and it will constantly come back to haunt you.'

He was so right. A few miles from us is a house that had a stunning copper beech in its front garden. It had huge silver arms and a glorious canopy and was admired by everyone who passed by. Unfortunately it had been planted much too close to the building and, as a result, this glorious tree was felled last year.

'Was it diseased?' I asked the owner.

'I hated taking it down but it blocked out the light from the house and the roots were beginning to damage the foundations. It just had to go – I still miss it, though.'

When we look at the garden now, some of our early mistakes are all too apparent, but this was always going to be the case given our limited knowledge. We planted two *Cupressus macrocarpa* 'Goldcrest' either side of the steps that lead down through the lawns and terraces in front of the house. We felt the aromatic, golden-yellow foliage, conical shape and fast growth would help to disguise the newness of the building. What we overlooked was our rule about carefully assessing the impact of microclimate and how this can change if any new planting or structures are introduced. The house channelled the wind around a corner and in winter the spot where the trees were planted began to face icy blasts. The very cold winter of 2010 carved great gaps in the foliage which have never fully recovered and we have been battling to make these two trees look respectable ever since. In the end they may still have to come down.

We console ourselves that we didn't succumb to the temptation of planting an excess of leylandii. In our eyes, the fashion for planting this very fast-growing conifer as hedging is perhaps the greatest planting error in modern times and it has certainly left its mark in this part of Ireland. Sites that were stripped of their native Irish hedges were often planted up with these vigorous conifers. Though they make good shelter belts and give quick privacy, they don't stop growing when they reach a height of six feet. Trimming is a never-ending task and, once they have got out of hand, thinning or total removal is a major headache. One neighbour facing the ever-expanding greenery surrounding his property found that his hedges had grown to be eleven feet wide and required drastic surgery. The specialist trimming was costly and within three years the whole process had to be repeated.

Planted as single trees in the right place, where there is ample room to expand, Leyland cypress or Castlewellan can be good additions to a garden – they provide quick cover and are cheap and widely available. We used them, along with laurel and holly, to provide the green tunnel we wanted to create just inside the gate from the road, and they quickly joined to form the canopy. We also planted half a dozen cheap container-grown leylandii along a ridge on one of our boundaries in the teeth of the prevailing winds and, although they were firmly staked, their shallow roots could not stand the winter gales and eventually they were all bent over. Since they were on the boundary we left them where they fell – they have since turned into an oddly shaped but thriving small spinney, a true testament to the vigour of these trees.

For variety, we also added to the bare-root oaks, rowan and willow wherever there seemed to be a space or we felt a small spinney might add to the landscape. With little real planning, we filled up odd corners by planting single specimens of

Chamaecyparis lawsoniana 'Intertexta', spruce, thuja and, on a wet spot, the rust-coloured swamp cypress. In addition, a friend who has a magnificent sixty-foot-high specimen of *Abies grandis* (grand fir) gave me half a dozen self-set offshoots that I placed in strategic locations around the garden. At first, we were really just trying to fill up the 'construction site' that we had created. This also led to an odd form of bargain hunting on our part. In contrast to the usual approach to buying plants – in which you look for the healthiest specimen – our strategy was to look in out-of-the-way corners of garden centres to see if there were trees that were pot-bound, ailing or damaged and then make a bid for them. Prices for these casualties – sickly specimens, which no self-respecting gardener would entertain – were often a fraction of the price of their healthy counterparts and we snapped them up. The reasoning was simple: if they eventually managed to recover, we had a bargain; if they died, no great loss.

At one point during this period, I spotted a skip filled with quite sizeable pot-grown trees as I arrived at the local garden centre.

'What's wrong with the trees in the skip?' I asked.

'Old stock that didn't sell, and now they've reached that size they never will. They are badly pot bound and beginning to die back so they're on the way to the tip. You can have them for your plot if you want to take a chance with them.'

I retrieved them quickly and, though they were all in a sorry state, I loaded all eight on to my trailer. None had labels but there seemed to be three leylandii, three different species of acer, one pyrus and one which the nursery man thought was a black walnut.

'Take this as well,' he said, handing me a sad-looking gingko tree. 'It's a maidenhair conifer but the bark on the trunk has been stripped by rabbits and I don't think it is salvageable.'

The rabbits had indeed chewed off most of the bark at ground level but a tiny strip remained so I threw it into the trailer too.

Back at the Fod, to try to restore the gingko, we stripped bark from one of the branches, fixed it around the damaged trunk with tape and planted it. It still survives – just – but only time will tell if it will eventually become a healthy tree. Like most gardeners, we live in hope! We planted the eight other trees as a future glade on the edge of what we hoped would become a wild flower meadow. For three years they looked a very miserable sight. During the fourth year they suddenly sprang into life and are now thriving specimens. We always had great fun with our cut-price scrounging; sometimes the results were outstanding and made us feel good both about the financial saving and the fact that we had managed to save trees from the bonfire or the dump.

Tree planting was always a pleasure but there were odd moments of frustration. Before we left Nottinghamshire, I went into Sherwood Forest to gather a few acorns from beneath the Major Oak as a memento of our old haunts. This is an ancient tree near the village of Edwinstowe and, according to local folklore, it the shelter where Robin Hood and his merry men slept. It has a girth of thirty-three feet and since Victorian times its massive limbs have been partially supported by an elaborate system of scaffolding. Only two of my six precious acorns grew and I proudly planted out the pair of tiny saplings, trying to imagine what they would look like a thousand years hence. One is now about six feet high, the other was eaten by a passing rabbit an hour after it was planted!

One afternoon, when I was planting three buddleia shrubs with a view to attracting butterflies, a member of the local gardening club arrived. He had very generously brought some hostas from his own garden. When he saw what I was doing, he gently challenged me on a point I hadn't previously considered.

'I thought you were trying to create a garden to attract local wildlife,' he said with a puzzled look.

'That's the hope, but it's still at the early stage, so who knows?'

'Surely if you want to attract native wildlife you have to use native plants. Buddleia comes originally from China.'

'The butterflies enjoy it,' I replied defensively, but his comment set me thinking about whether or not we should be concentrating our efforts on planting only native species. Since we had already planted bamboo, Austrian pine, sycamore and many other species from around the world his comment rankled a little and I wondered if we had made a serious mistake in our plant selection.

On reflection, we decided that it mattered little where any plant originates – what is important is whether or not it meets the needs of the species we hope to attract. In any case it is astonishingly difficult to ascertain which plants are truly native and which have been brought to these islands at some time in the past and are blow-ins. Species have been moved around for centuries by settlers or collectors and it constantly comes as a surprise to discover the precise origins of so-called native plants. Furthermore, anyone with a bird table will know that the finches, tits and sparrows that visit daily seem to care little that the peanuts and sunflower seeds that they enjoy so much came originally from the Americas. It is true, though, that certain species are very choosy about their needs: red admirals may enjoy the nectar from buddleia but still need native nettles on which to lay their eggs and devil's-bit scabious is essential for the survival of the marsh fritillary butterfly, but being too dogmatic in the 'native/ non-native' argument is pointless. What really matters is whether or not what you are planting works for local wildlife.

Our friend, Jim Whiteside the retired forestry man, helped our understanding of what to plant by informing us that some trees hold more insect life than others – oak is the best followed by birch, willow, silver birch and hawthorn. Alder, poplar and beech are also useful, as is rowan with its berries. Of course, nothing is ever simple, though, as a belt of firs – although conspicuously absent from this list – can provide shelter and winter roosts. As with most things, a variety is probably best. As Jim put it, 'You pays your money and you takes your choice!'

Our need to try to create this garden without it costing the earth also led us, as complete beginners, to consider trying to expand our planting by the use of home-grown trees and shrubs. Andrew Donnelly at the Moy nursery had suggested we thicken up the edge of one spinney with dogwood and had supplied us with six red and six yellow bare-root plants. These flourished. He had also instructed us to cut them back hard in spring, both to promote better winter colour and also to thicken up the plants. Rather than putting the cuttings on to the compost heap we pushed them all well down into damp ground and, much to our amazement, virtually all of them grew. This was the first time we realised that this part of Ireland, with its continuously damp soil, is first class for striking cuttings and since that discovery we have tried this method with pretty much everything. Willows, alders, laurel and the dogwood eventually multiplied from a few specimens to dozens.

In the first three or four months of this project we had planted several hundred whips and assorted shrubs, but the plot – with the exception of the outside borders where there was a belt of mature ash – still looked barren and uninviting. The heavy machinery that had been used for the draining and lake building had also left its mark. The bleak appearance of the land was made much worse when I arrived one morning to find that someone had dumped seven black bin bags of rubbish over the hedge. Though it looked as though these had been knotted and sealed, foxes had torn up three bags and the contents had been scattered by the wind over a wide area. The land looked like a municipal tip and we were both infuriated that anyone could think it acceptable to drive out to the countryside, find a quiet lane where no one was about and throw their refuse over the nearest hedge. This discovery was especially galling because in the next village there is a council recycling centre where anyone can dispose of rubbish easily and legitimately.

Seething with anger, I began to gather up the debris. As I did so, I noticed that prescriptions, bills and old envelopes all had the same address. One of the sacks was still intact but when I opened it, its contents clearly came from the same house. I phoned the council to report what had happened, loaded the re-sealed bags into the back of the four-by-four and set off to find the culprit. I soon arrived at a house on a crescent with neat open-plan front gardens and well-manicured lawns. A woman came to the door when I knocked.

'I've brought your rubbish back,' I said, with a black bag in either hand.

'I don't know what you mean,' she said. 'That's not my rubbish!'

'Well it all has your address and plenty of the stuff is only a few days old.'

I emptied one of the sacks on to her rockery.

'There's utility bills, packaging and envelopes all with your address. See for yourself.'

I tipped the second sack on to the rose bed.

'And there's more in the car,' and I pulled the other bags from the vehicle and scattered them on to her lawn.

'Not very pretty is it?' I said, feeling much better as I drove off.

It would be wonderful to say that this careless disregard for the countryside was a one-off, but over the next few years we came to realise that this kind of behaviour was far too common. The narrow country lanes in this part of Tyrone are lovely and none more so than the one which runs through the centre of nearby Seskinore Forest. Mature deciduous trees arch over the road and form a spectacular leaf canopy through which dappled light sparkles, giving the whole place a magical quality. Strolling through this ancient woodland is always something special and it comes as a shock to find that someone has discarded the complete wrappings and drink cans from a takeaway meal on to the banks of violets and celandines. At certain times of the year this behaviour is quite commonplace – so much so that when Rosemary takes the dogs on their regular circuit around the forest, she always carries a bag to collect the litter. It is also astonishing just how much rubbish is jettisoned from passing vehicles. Wine bottles, cigarette cartons, snack and takeaway junk is dumped without thought on to the verges of wonderful lanes and until it is picked up acts as a depressing commentary on modern attitudes. One other walker who also tidies up as she goes put it well, 'We may now have better houses and flashier cars but if we have not learnt to have more regard for our countryside we still have a long way to go!'

Perhaps even more surprising are the actions of some farmers. Sheep and cattle carcasses are regularly found dumped in ditches alongside these forestry lanes. Identifying marks have always been removed, and the animals are left to stink and rot where they were thrown. Farmers have to pay for the removal of dead animals so, apparently, some unscrupulous people drive to one of these quiet spots alongside the forestry and discard the remains. The forest authorities are then obliged to remove them from their property. This distasteful practice on the part of a few rogue farmers is upsetting, especially since the tourist board are spending a fortune trying to promote these lanes as havens – perfect for walking, cycling and horse riding. The practice also reflects badly on the hundreds of farmers who dispose of animal carcasses responsibly and who deplore this kind of behaviour.

This total disregard for conservation and the preservation of our rural heritage was illustrated at one stage during our early days at the Fod. One local man began to dump lorry loads of waste on to one section of the nearby raised bog. Although the ownership of the land was disputed, he certainly had no permission for landfill, but a steady stream of lorries suddenly began to arrive up the ancient bog lane laden with all kinds of waste. The loads were deposited on to the pristine raised bogland which had previously been undisturbed for centuries and to make things worse, few local people seemed in any way perturbed by this development. The new dump was adjacent to our land and one morning when I was walking across it, I found material discarded from the local hospital. This discovery instantly brought matters to a head and the offender was taken to court and made to stop. It wasn't the ownership or otherwise of the land or the nature of the material being dumped which bothered us both, but the fact that so many people thought it acceptable to abuse a scarce and valuable ecosystem in this way. Once these raised boglands are destroyed they are gone forever, and the flora and fauna they support goes with them.

On the lower land adjacent to the recently constructed lakes we hoped to establish a wild flower meadow. In our mind's eye we saw an area of poppies, cornflowers and buttercups, with insects and butterflies flitting about everywhere – really we planned to create our own 'bee-loud glade'. This dream was the stuff of childhood reading books, romantic rural calendars and advertisements that portray a stylised, nostalgic view of the countryside. The reality is very different. Modern farming has wiped out these dream landscapes and the acres of dense ryegrass, swathes of sugar beet and chemical-drenched cereal fields make it virtually impossible to find even a single wild flower, never mind a thriving meadow. It is true that the odd field of buttercups still remains and, in the wilder western reaches of Ireland, unimproved pasture can still be found, but overall the ancient meadows of the past have gone – only 2 per cent of those that existed in 1949 remain.

As with so many aspects of our project, we hoped to reverse this dismal trend, but in reality it proved much more difficult than we had imagined. Many gardening pundits make the process of establishing a meadow sound relatively easy, but in practice the glib advice offered is often of little help to the beginner.

'*Wild flowers thrive on poor soil so if you have rich soil, skim off the top layer.*' Possible no doubt for the corner of a small garden, but for an acre and a half? I don't think so. It was true that our fields had been badly treated over the years but, like most of the land around, had also been subject to the annual dose of nitrogen and repeated showers of slurry. The land may have been wet but it was also nutrient rich. The combination of old ryegrass and fertiliser meant that, even if left to their own devices, very few wild flowers appeared and any we planted were soon swamped.

'*Cut the meadow in autumn and remove all of the grass.*' There is of course sound logic behind this advice in that if the grass is removed, the fertility is reduced year by year. Coarse plants will eventually do less well and the wild flowers will have a chance to thrive. Unfortunately in our case it was difficult to get a tractor and mower into the meadow and even trickier to see and negotiate around the small trees we had planted. Grass and vegetation at the end of the growing season was just too big a challenge for the ride-on mower and though a scythe may be nostalgically attractive, using one on an acre and a half is a sure recipe for blistered hands and a dodgy back, even if I did know how to use one!

'*Buy wild flower seed mixes that suit your geographical location and soil type.*' Sensible – but wild flower seed is very expensive and, for the acre-and-a-half we had in mind, buying enough to make an impact was out of the question. To illustrate the point, the local council eschewed planting the usual bedding plants and instead sowed a wild flower patch on a nearby traffic island. It looked fantastic. I phoned the head gardener to ask his advice on how to proceed with our meadow.

'Rotivate or plough in spring and then sow the wild flower mix. Do not use any fertiliser and you should get a good show,' he said, which was all encouraging until he continued, 'I warn you, though, the seed is costly. It cost four thousand pounds for us to establish the meadow on that small piece of land.'

End of conversation!

The development of the meadow really did illustrate the level of our gardening expertise. We had planted a crab apple tree on the edge of the wild flower area as we felt it would be in keeping with the landscape and might eventually provide some feeding for the blackbirds. We carefully pruned and shaped the tree, following closely the advice given in the gardening books, and as it matured we often stood back and admired our efforts.

'Making a fine-looking tree,' I said. 'Should have a good crop of crab apples next year.'

It did indeed fruit well the following year and has done so ever since. Though not with crab apples but Victoria plums!

In the end we stopped worrying about trying to copy the meadows in the gardening books and left things to nature. We scattered seeds from primrose, cowslips and red campion in hedge bottoms and on banks and, though the return per seed was surprisingly poor, some specimens did emerge and hopefully will eventually spread. Buttercups, knapweed, purple loosestrife and meadowsweet soon appeared and the yellow rattle we had planted seemed to be spreading. It was beginning to look and feel like a proper meadow, especially once butterflies, moths and bees began to arrive. So did substantial numbers of mice and shrews, which was something we had not anticipated at this stage.

The first honey bee I spotted tempted me to sign up for a beekeeping course. At that time I naively thought that there were only two kinds of bee in the UK and Ireland – the bumble bee and the honey bee – and it came as a real surprise to find there are in fact over 250. True, not all of them are found in our part of Northern Ireland, and distinguishing one species from another can be difficult, but all have a vital part to play in any habitat so signing up to learn more about them seemed a worthwhile venture. The trouble was that the instructor on the course turned out to be the sort of person who could crush the enthusiasm of the keenest of students. In a few weeks I went from wanting to learn everything about bees to being content to buy a pot of honey in Lidl. He would arrive (usually late), take off his hat to reveal a hairless head like a shiny wet stone, preen his NIM (walrus-like Northern Ireland Moustache, now only ever seen here or in Serbia), open his battered folder and read nonstop for two hours. We were bombarded with pages of unfathomable technical jargon, and introduced to the seemingly endless ways by which individual bees and their colonies could be wiped out. It soon felt that if you wanted to remain sane the whole process was best avoided. Why do some people think that droning on (no pun intended!) for weeks on end without ever establishing the level of understanding and prior knowledge of their audience constitutes good teaching? This chap obviously knew plenty about bees, but knew absolutely nothing about teaching and learning.

It was a painful experience and one evening before he could begin his normal spiel I asked, 'When do we get to see a hive and a real bee? Wouldn't the whole thing be easier for us to understand if you brought in a frame and a hive tool?'

He was instantly offended. 'I've been teaching this course for years now and no one has ever complained.'

'I expect they were all asleep,' I replied, having already decided that I wouldn't be returning.

The whole sorry episode reminded me of an experience I had suffered in a classroom years before, when I had been asked to observe a young science teacher and give an appraisal on the quality of his teaching. It had been a less-than-riveting session and the sixteen-year-old student sitting next to me at the back of the class had doodled away looking totally bored for the whole hour. When the bell went to end the torture, I turned to her and said, 'I have to make a note of the key learning objective of that lesson. What is the one thing you will take away from today?'

'The one thing I've learned?'

'Yes.'

'If I ever get married I'll never let a man of mine go out wearing a tie like that teacher's wearing!'

As with the case of Sal and the river studies, there is often a massive gap between what we think we are teaching and what the student is actually learning!

A few weeks later I was introduced to a local beekeeper who rigged me up with suit and hood and taught me more in half an hour about honey bees than I had learnt in the previous six weeks! We have still not got around to setting up our own hives but maybe some day.

One warm summer evening, just before dusk, I was standing at the edge of the new meadow watching the insect life and moths flitting about above the purple knapweed and feeling pretty pleased with things when something truly memorable occurred. A barn owl ghosted in, hunted the edge of the meadow before turning a few feet from me and lifting silently over the nearest hedge. What a sight! What a moment! We learned later from the Barn Owl Trust that this had been the first sighting in the area in thirty years.

5

More Formal Moves

Style in gardening is a very personal thing and what is a joy to the eye for one person, rankles with others. Our garden in Sherwood Forest was a secret garden, surrounded by huge beeches and oaks, and contained along one side by a high ivy-covered wall. It was part country-house style, with clipped box, holly and yew, and part cottage garden with perennial-filled pots and a profusion of annuals and herbs. We always loved this variety but particularly liked the fact that we could walk from the formal garden directly into the woodland proper without having to negotiate any noticeable boundary or fence. The garden simply merged into the woodland beyond, giving us a feeling of being part of a natural world which had remained largely unchanged for centuries. We longed to replicate this feeling of belonging in our Irish garden design, so that as things matured, we would have something which would merge seamlessly into the surrounding countryside without any discernible break. From our research and garden visits, we were now confident that the variety of habitat was the key to attracting wildlife, so we decided that we would strive for more manicured and formal planting around the house, with the plan that the garden would become less formal and more natural looking as we moved out towards the boundaries.

One other hope with the garden design was that we could create something that would be impossible to see in its entirety at a single glance when it matured. It would have hidden spots, pathways that led to other areas and surprise vistas that suddenly opened up as the walker reached them. Wildlife habitat would always be our prime aim, but if it were possible to build elements into the design that prompted intrigue and curiosity then that would be a bonus.

We also wanted to make sure that we would be able to watch birds and animals from the house, rather than needing to go outside every time. During our period of visiting older houses in the area, we noticed that many had no view of the garden, river or landscape in which they stood. Windows were so high that it was impossible to see out of them, and badly positioned sheds or farm buildings often blocked any interesting views. So, with this in mind, we constructed a traditional tower at the front of the house, which gave panoramic views across the country and which provided a perfect upstairs spot for morning tea and toast. We also made sure that all the downstairs windows were low enough so that we could see the landscape when seated. The terraced lawns that ran down to the lake were also carefully angled so that their height did not obscure the view to the water.

We finally moved into the house in June 2004 and were delighted with the solitude. Much of the time there was no sound of human activity and, though at this time there was little wildlife to watch, we could see the potential of the garden. Coming from England, I had not realised how long the summer days would be and how early the sun comes up in the mornings – though, disappointingly, the dawn chorus was still largely absent despite our early work in the garden.

We did have some surprises. One warm summer night the bedroom windows were wide open and we heard a series of weird noises floating up from the new lakes. There were strangulated piglet-like squeals, odd whistling notes and single chipping noises that seemed really loud and went on for most of the night. The sounds were repeated every night after that, beginning each evening just as dusk was falling, continuing all night and then stopping at first light. We had no idea what kind of creature was making these odd sounds and – in the pitch black of the night –

couldn't make anything out, even with the night scope.

The answer came one afternoon a few weeks later when we were sitting by one of the new lakes and marvelling at the rate at which the vegetation was cloaking the bare soil on the banks. Rosemary spotted some kind of small chick running across a gap in the reeds. I focused the binoculars and kept them trained on the spot she mentioned.

Two more tiny long-legged chicks dashed past. They had me puzzled until an adult bird appeared, hesitated a second and disappeared into the reeds after the chicks. The long red bill thrust forward like a sword was the giveaway and I immediately knew what had been making the noises at night – water rails!

Though these secretive water birds are widespread in the swampy parts of Ireland, seeing one is a rare treat. They seldom emerge from the reed beds and if disturbed will fly only a short distance before dropping back into cover. It is a pity they are so difficult to see because they are handsome birds with their mottled, slate-grey plumage and long, vivid red bills. They are nervous and shy and we both knew we might have a long wait before seeing another one out in the open.

We were also thrilled to spot house martins wheeling and soaring through the air that first summer and had high hopes that they would begin to nest. We had purposely built wide eaves in the hope that they would find these suitable, and had even placed some artificial nests on the house, but none chose to build that first year. We were already learning that patience is a vital attribute when it comes to anything to do with wildlife.

Even though the part of the garden near the house still looked like a construction site, we held the faith and started to plan the best places from which to enjoy the garden as it matured. Without doubt the sunniest, most sheltered part of the garden was one particular spot in front of the kitchen window to the south-west of the house. This had sunshine all day until early evening and was protected at its rear from the prevailing winds by the ridge of land, and a mature belt of surrounding ash and larch. This was clearly the place to sit and we decided to build a sizeable circular patio, which consisted of small concrete pavers with a ring of rust-coloured edging stones. The construction looked decidedly isolated and odd, sitting out in the middle of an empty field with nothing planted around it, and it always prompted questions from first-time visitors. One driver delivering blocks and cement saw it and asked our builders what it was. Quick as a flash one of them replied, 'It's a helipad. Owner of this place hates travelling by car.'

We lost track of how many times after that we heard someone refer to the place with the helipad. Who needs Facebook or the internet when the rural telegraph is so efficient?

Years later when the patio was enclosed by trellis, rambling roses and honeysuckle, I was sitting there, having tea and cake with an elderly neighbour when he asked, 'How did you know to build a place to sit on this precise spot?'

'It's where the sun strikes and it is the most sheltered place in the whole garden. Why do you ask?'

'Because when I was a lad and we picked spuds here this is the exact place we used to come to eat our sandwiches and get a drop of tea.'

In truth, deciding where to place seats became something of an obsession. Sitting still is easily the best way to observe the comings and goings in the countryside and, although our arrival with the dogs causes some disturbance, we are always struck by how quickly the birds and animals seem to forget us and revert to their daily routines once we're sitting. We decided to put seats at the sunny spots near to the house, next to the ponds, in the growing woodlands and along the side of the meadow. Sometimes these were elegant cast-iron, restored Victorian benches but usually they were just wooden stakes driven into the ground and topped with a length of old scaffolding plank. One visiting gardener surprised me when he said, 'I've counted eighteen seats around your garden – was that deliberate?'

'Yes,' I said. 'It's what this kind of garden should be about. Taking time to look and listen and it helps if there are places to sit.'

He nodded in agreement and immediately sat down on the nearest bench!

At one stage in the building process, when Lawrence was excavating the footings of the house, he unearthed a huge whitish quartz stone, which we decided to incorporate into the garden design. Rosemary and I share the view that less is more when it comes to garden ornaments as they can quickly make a garden look like a churchyard, but we felt that two statues would give some added interest to the more formal part of the plot. This large stone came as an unexpected bonus, and we decided to use it to raise the height of one of the statues we had in mind. The plan was to place a statue, probably a figure, in the centre of a circle of thuya firs, and use this as a focal point at the end of an avenue of purple-leaved *Prunus cerasifera* 'Nigra' trees.

The trouble was that authentic, weathered antiques from the specialist dealers were very costly. In the end we decided to stretch to one genuine old piece and one modern reproduction. The antique had the patina of age; we used yogurt and sour milk on the new statue to hasten the ageing process and make it look more in keeping with the style of the house.

In fact buying the statues made us realise just how expensive pots and garden ornaments had become since we last needed them. The place we had left in Nottinghamshire had been equipped with what we considered to be the correct number of patio pots and tubs. We left some behind as they seemed part of the garden but as we had purchased most of these years ago, we were shocked at the outlay needed to buy similar new ones. Equipping a garden, especially one the size of ours, was an expense we had not anticipated. Since we were developing the garden on a shoestring we had to seek another solution and found it in a building materials salvage yard just over the border at Lifford. The place was an Aladdin's cave of old stone, concrete pots, plinths, bird baths and indeed anything ornamental that might have graced gardens for the past fifty to a hundred years. There were goblins, leprechauns, frogs and concrete pigs by the barrow load. Most of it was junk but amongst the clutter was the occasional hidden gem. On one occasion Rosemary unearthed two larger-than-life stone grouse, wonderfully weathered, and asked the owner the price. 'Fifteen euros each,' he said.

'You mean twenty euros for the pair?' she asked.

'Maths wasn't your strongest subject at school, was it? Go on, take them for ten each,' he said, smiling.

It was good business because over the years we have gone back to buy pots, urns, troughs, and all manner of bits and bobs.

We got into the way of hunting for discarded items to which we could give a new lease of life, and some finds became truly memorable. Jim Riddell – our farming neighbour of the 'rhyming slang' fame – turned up with the carcass of an old Victorian postbox, which had lain in one of his barns for years.

'It was in the wall outside my house from before I was born,' he said, 'but was exchanged when it was damaged. The small door at the front has gone and parts have rusted a bit but you should be able to restore it. It will look the part at your house.'

Rosemary's brother, Kevin, a man adept at rebuilding old tractors or indeed anything else in need of attention, made it a new door, cleaned the metal and re-sprayed it in traditional pillar-box red. We built it into a brick pillar outside the kitchen window, and it looks superb.

Oddly enough, this postbox was responsible for our first 'challenge' from the local wildlife. Most days, we unlocked the postbox and took out the letters within hours of them being delivered, but when we were away for a few days we noticed that many of the envelopes were shredded, like a mini strimmer had moved over them. Initially I suspected mice but one day I noticed a snail on one of the inside walls and felt around the box to discover some twenty more fixed to the inner top and sides. To this day I have no idea why the postbox is so popular with these molluscs but reaching inside every few days and removing the latest squatters has become part of my routine.

On another occasion we thought a stone plinth would give some point of focus amongst the growing shrubbery but there was nothing suitable in the salvage yard and prices in the garden centre were just too high for an item that wasn't essential. They say 'necessity is the mother of invention' so we decided on an optical illusion: we found a four-foot length of old concrete drainage pipe, stood it upright on a square lid from a cattle drinking trough, coiled a rope dipped in wet mortar around the stem and topped it with another lid. Close up it looked very rough but at a distance it did the job perfectly. Total cost, two pounds.

Seeking out our few reclaimed ornaments also brought amusement. When I spotted that first barn owl over the meadow we thought we would commemorate the occasion by trying to find a stone owl in the salvage yard. After half an hour of searching through the piles of junk, I finally spotted a nicely weathered barn owl and pulled it triumphantly from the heap. At first glance it looked perfect – beautifully modelled feathers, head turned to one side, cost minimal – but, unfortunately, when I turned it round it was playing a banjo.

Over the years we have accumulated a wide range of containers and pots, some antiques, some new, and though they look wonderful in summer with their geraniums, begonias and colourful annuals, they do require maintenance, care and commitment. The daily watering, dead-heading and weeding needed to keep them looking their best is pleasurable in a small garden but can become a chore when there are so many other tasks. We always aimed to make the garden as manageable as possible but perhaps, as beginners, did not fully appreciate how much work is involved just to keep even the containers and pots looking reasonably cared for.

The lawns are a good example of the way in which we underestimated how much time the garden would demand of us. We had noticed that on any dry day in summer, mowers are out in every garden in Ireland. Before we bought our site, I remember saying that I didn't want to spend every spare minute cutting grass – our intention was to have the minimum expanse of lawn. Where possible, we planned to cut narrow paths for walking and leave the rest to become meadowland. Things didn't work out that way. The terraces down to the lakes looked untidy and too informal if left, although we kept telling ourselves they would be better for any wildlife. Aesthetically, letting the grass grow became impossible to live with. And, although the return of the wildlife was the primary aim, gardens have to be multi-purpose. Parts of them are outside living rooms, to be used and enjoyed by people as well as wildlife, and their design has to be flexible enough to accommodate this. If the design is too formal and the planting too delicate, there is no space for football and fun, and proper relaxation is more difficult for everyone. As an example, on high days and holidays in the summer – when our sons, daughters-in-law and grandchildren visit – we roll out sixty yards of plastic sheeting from the front of the house, over the terraces and down to the lake. A constant water supply from the hosepipe and regular doses of washing- up liquid make sure that the body boards really pick up some speed. On other occasions we use one of the lawns for croquet – impossible with long grass! Worrying about what these activities are doing to the garden would certainly detract from their enjoyment.

Luckily, our acreage is large enough for a mixture of true meadowland and formal lawns. We have never used weed killers, top dressing or fertilisers and have learnt to live with the mosses, daisies and dandelions that appeared. It is easy to become obsessed with achieving lawn perfection, and trying to get rid of moss in Ireland, where the rainfall can be significant and the land poorly drained, is expensive, unrelenting and a battle that is difficult to win. It is much less stressful and better for wildlife to admit defeat and enjoy a mossy lawn.

Planning and planting the formal garden in front of the kitchen window has not been our greatest gardening success. We tried to abide by our original principles of putting in plants and shrubs that would be attractive to wildlife, and went for things that would provide berries, nectar or shelter, but our knowledge and understanding of herbaceous gardening was clearly not up to the task of creating something harmonious and long-lasting. We planted many of the perennials in the wrong place and consequently they grew too large and straggly, were swamped or died off thanks to the heavy land. At the height of summer the border does attract plenty of butterflies and birds but it always looks confused and haphazard. Fourteen years after we started this section of the garden, it can best be described as a work in progress and we are still experimenting with the most suitable arrangements of perennials and shrubs.

Brian, one of the joiners working on the house, no doubt noticing that this part of the garden lacked planning, built a substantial bird table for us and followed it a few weeks later with a fantastic dovecote. These welcome additions did seem to give more structure to the plot. The generosity of this joiner is a good example of the way the whole team of builders got fully behind our aim of trying to bring wildlife back to the area. Throughout the building process the builders asked us all the time about our long-term aims, what species we hoped to attract and what we intended to do with this or that part of the land, and it was clear that there was a genuine interest in making it all happen.

We realised early on that a young garden such as ours lacked the natural holes found in mature trees that birds need and that a range of nest boxes might provide an artificial substitute. Initially we erected boxes that would suit blue tits, great tits and robins and placed them in secluded positions above head height and facing towards the east. They had mixed fortunes. Some were of interest immediately and, in one case, a pair of great tits were in and out of the box within hours of it going up. Every gardener or wildlife enthusiast knows there is something truly exciting and satisfying about watching blue tits or great tits ferrying food for their young backwards and forwards to a nest box you have erected. Enjoyable too because the caterpillars or bugs they are carrying are some of the less desirable characters that invade cabbages or rosebushes. Other boxes were never inspected or used so we moved them to different locations after several unproductive years.

Even a local birdwatching expert couldn't give a definitive answer as to why some boxes were used and some weren't. 'They can be in a position which is too sunny or they can be in a territory which is already occupied by rivals. Even the wrong kind of varnish or preservative can put the birds off. Sometimes the local habitat just doesn't have the right food supply nearby so move them round till you find a location the birds like.'

It turns out that bird boxes are another element in the wildlife garden for which trial and error is the best policy.

To surround the more 'formal' parts of the garden, we again began by selecting a range of shrubs that we hoped would be attractive to wildlife. Berberis, buddleia, flowering currant, firethorn, heather, lavender, holly and viburnum were cheap and available so formed the bulk of our early purchases. We used honeysuckle, climbing roses, ivy and golden hop for the trellising around the patio, along with a crab apple tree for height. With little thought for colour combinations or size, we went for a mixture of chives, campions, dahlias, fennel, foxgloves, Michaelmas daisies, lupins and sunflowers to fill the barren ground in front the kitchen window – on the principle that the more plants we grew, the more insects we were likely to attract, we piled them in. Real gardeners would probably be appalled at our lack of planning but, at the time, it seemed that getting something growing in the space was what mattered and that more sophisticated, better plans could come later. With hindsight, I now think that it would have been better to have started with a proper herbaceous plan and to have shown patience in waiting for the beds to mature, rather than putting something in when it became available and hoping that it was in the right place.

Taking a chance sometimes paid off though. One winter day, the local nurseryman gave me a tree that he thought was past its prime with the words, 'I'm not sure what this is but take it if you have a spare spot.'

I placed it in the 'formal' part of the garden alongside the bordering laurel hedge and it turned out to be a catalpa. With pure luck it finished up in a very sheltered spot that suited it perfectly. It has since matured into a terrific tree that, with its huge leaves, really does give an exotic feel to that corner of the patch. Every winter I am fearful that the frosts have finished it off because many of the outer limbs look dead, but once warmer spring days arrive, the tiny purple buds sprout again and grow magnificently into the characteristic light green trowel-like leaves.

Equally often our bargain-hunting strategy well and truly backfired. We had the bright idea that some daffodils planted under the new trees would in time spread and give interest in spring when this part of Tyrone can look a little dull. I contacted a Dutch bulb company and the conversation went like this.

'I'm looking for a few daffodils to plant on the edge of new woodlands. What do you suggest?'

'Carlton will do well and should suit your location. They are not too tall so won't be affected by strong winds. How many do you need?'

'A couple of hundred should do for a start.'

'The price is much better if you buy them by the sack.'

'How many are in a sack?'

'Approximately five hundred – but if you take four sacks there is no postal charge and the rate per bulb is very competitive.'

That's how we came to plant two thousand daffodil bulbs in the pouring rain one bitterly cold November day, mud sticking to everything, telling ourselves the true pleasure of gardening comes from delayed gratification.

When the spring finally comes round and the banks of daffodils are in full bloom the hard work involved with planting is instantly forgotten and I have my annual conversation with the bulb wholesaler usually with the same end result. At the moment we have put in eight thousand bulbs. Who knows where it will all end?

The final part of the hard structural plan for the garden involved building steps down the slopes of the two terraces from the front of the house. We bordered these with mixed conifer hedging and Portuguese laurel, and completed the pathway that led down to one of the newly created lakes with support arches for climbing roses. At the rear of the house we built an enclosed courtyard with a greenhouse and open-sided covered area. We had in mind a sheltered place that would be useful for entertaining or eating outdoors during the summer months. The shaded wall was planted up with ivy, the sunniest wall with a pear tree and a range of patio pots with herbs completed the picture. We fitted a 'sparrow terrace' to the shaded wall and hoped this might, in some small way, help to stem the huge population decline house sparrows have suffered in recent years. It is estimated that the current UK numbers of this bird have dropped to half what they were in the 1980s and the cause is unclear. Clearance of old buildings and a reduction of the bird's traditional nesting sites is thought to be partly responsible so provision of suitable nest boxes might help. House sparrows are very sociable birds and like to live in compact colonies so a number of boxes joined together like terraced housing is a pattern they seem to find attractive. On the other side of the courtyard we had fingers crossed that the open rafters of the lean-to shelter would eventually attract swallows. This soon happened but the arrival of nesting swallows brought us our second conflict with wildlife. We used the open–sided area for drying laundry on a mobile clothes line, and sheets, towels and shirts don't sit well under nests full of feeding swallow chicks. The clothes line had to move to the garage – that's commitment to conservation for you!

As a family, we have always loved cooking, so we were keen to grow our own vegetables. We had chosen a spot that was exactly right in terms of the position of the sun, but it was very wet and the soil was heavy and sticky. We put in land drains and raised the beds with old scaffolding planks. We made three sizeable compost bays from discarded palettes with the plan of working to a three-year cycle: fill one bay with the garden rubbish, leaves and so on; leave this to mature for two years while filling the next bay; and then put all of the matured three-year-old compost on to the raised vegetable beds. As the vegetable plot was close to open countryside we decided to erect a rabbit-proof fence around the plot, although we hadn't spotted many rabbits at this stage.

To begin with results were dismal and it would have made more sense to buy the vegetables we were attempting to grow. But as the soil improved, so did the crops, and now, during the summer and autumn, we are 'self-providing'. We use that term because total self-sufficiency is incredibly difficult for amateurs to achieve and, in order to avoid a feeling of failure when we need to buy in vegetables, it is perhaps better not to aim too high! The real motivation for our 'grow your own' initiative was to try to get vegetables that were totally organic. In Nottinghamshire our neighbouring farmer grew produce for the city and supplied the markets with a succession of broccoli, cabbage, carrots and spring onions. He sprayed regularly and one day I asked him if it was wise to drench the crops a few days before they went to market. His answer changed our thinking entirely: 'Most sprays are systemic and soak into the vegetables.'

'So you can't wash them off?'

'No.'

'Do you eat the vegetables you grow?'

'Not the ones in the field. We grow our own organics in a plot behind the house.'

We grow lots of our favourite vegetables with a fair degree of success, but have less luck with carrots. Every year we try them, and once every three years we get a half-decent crop, but normally they fail and I don't know why. Even the rabbits refuse to eat my carrots. However optimism is an essential prerequisite for all gardeners so we keep trying. Though our produce may not be perfect, at least we know there is nothing harmful inside!

As every gardener knows, growing courgettes is a mixed blessing. They seem to thrive in Ireland: suddenly every plant sprouts bright yellow flowers and from that point onward using all the courgettes is a challenge. It seems to take only a matter of hours before yet another batch is ready and we have tried almost every recipe to try to keep pace with the glut: soup, gratin, curry and many other variations but in the end we always lose the race and finish up with a surfeit of full-blown marrows. Now we know some devotees argue stuffed marrow or marrow jam is worth making but in our view the end result hardly justifies the effort involved. One year we hit on a solution. Cut the marrow in half with a spade and leave it on the vegetable patch. Within hours the blackbirds have stripped the flesh clean and left only the tough outer skins. Wildlife to the rescue again.

So there it was. By autumn 2005 we had come from buying five acres of wet, barren land and dreaming about creating a wildlife garden, to moving into the house and seeing the rudiments of our plan begin to take shape. We had thickened up the existing hedges with parallel plantings, put in over a thousand deciduous trees and conifers, excavated two lakes and a small pond and begun the process of establishing a wild flower meadow. In the formal garden we had set out hedges of beech, laurel, privet and Portuguese laurel and had planted a range of shrubs and perennials that we hoped would prove attractive to wildlife. We'd added a vegetable plot and orchard at the rear of the house. We hoped that the house and courtyard, built in traditional Irish country style, would eventually lose their newness and would blend in once they weathered and the surrounding trees softened the stark outlines. We hoped that even the formal gardens and indeed the buildings would in time become an important part of the habitat we dreamt of creating. The stage was set and it was now a matter of waiting to find out if any of the local wildlife wanted to be part of the cast.

6

First Arrivals

First we noticed the frogs. A few to begin with in a corner of the middle lake but, within days, dozens of mating pairs and glutinous masses of frogspawn filled one of the bays. The first few males uttered a faint croaking song but, once joined by hundreds of others, the complete ensemble could be heard at some distance and sounded like the gentle revving of a motorbike. Following the frogs the herons appeared, often several at a time, flapping in like prehistoric relics, to stand motionless until an unlucky frog came within range. Heronries have been thoroughly mapped across Northern Ireland and we knew from this data that there was a thriving colony some two miles away. Mature herons are noted for their detailed local knowledge of productive feeding spots and the birds are quick to add any new places to their daily search for food. They are patient assassins, prepared to stand for hours until a chance comes in range. When it does, their lunge with sword-like beak is lightning fast and few targets escape their deadly thrust.

Interestingly, plastic herons are often sold to garden pond owners to protect goldfish and carp – the theory being that if one heron is in residence others will be deterred. On our ponds, the opposite seemed to be the case and one heron attracted others. At the height of the frog-breeding season there were often as many as six herons stalking the margins and they frequently worked within yards of each other. The way wildlife behaves in practice often contradicts accepted folklore and, though the garden centre herons may be sold to deter others, the truth is they probably announce, 'there is something good on the menu so why not come and join us?'

Buzzards arrived next. Four of them watching and waiting on the ash tree overlooking the lake. Any frog that hopped from the shelter of the grassland to the water was seized by the nearest bird, lifted up to the top of a fence post, dispatched and eaten. The feast went on for days and, though some people might not like to see nature in the raw, it was fascinating to observe the behaviour of these spectacular birds. Their increased presence across Northern Ireland provokes a mixed reaction, as I learned one day when a friend and I were fixing the wire strainers to a fence. The mewing call of buzzards from the sky caused us both to look up. Rising pockets of warm air had carried three birds almost out of sight and they were tracing lazy circles high above us. Their free-floating silhouettes created an illusion of small eagles and the spectacle immediately captured our attention but in very different ways.

'What a magnificent sight,' I said. 'Surely the next best thing to seeing a real eagle.'

'Far too many of them about,' replied my friend. 'Something needs to be done. They do a lot of damage – especially to game.'

My companion was echoing the correspondence frequently seen in the sporting press that argues that buzzards are becoming too numerous, and should be taken off the protected list because they take too many reared pheasants. This is the kind of spurious logic that gives the sport of shooting a bad name. Undoubtedly buzzards do occasionally lift young pheasants, but their normal diet consists primarily of carrion, especially road kills, rabbits, a range of insects, worms and in early spring, as we have seen first-hand, spawning frogs. To destroy these magnificent raptors merely to save a few pheasants that will be shot a few weeks later makes no sense and the logic of this argument would certainly not be supported by conservationists and most people who shoot.

In my youth there was a specially erected wire fence alongside every gamekeeper's house that displayed rows and rows of rotting prey for all to see – these gibbets announced to the world that the keeper was doing his job and the predators on the estate were being efficiently shot or trapped. Modern sportsmen and indeed all lovers of the countryside would be horrified to see the range of species that fell victim to this persecution, but at the time the shooting of owls, kestrels, merlin, sparrowhawks, peregrines and buzzards was commonplace – accepted and indeed demanded by many landowners. If it was black and had a hooked beak or talons it was deemed a legitimate quarry, and the widespread practice of using baited traps, pole traps, poison and all-year-round shooting made the birds extinct in many parts. Happily attitudes have changed and today most people are much more enlightened as to which predators, if any, do any real harm and which deserve our absolute protection.

Life outside our wildlife project continued apace. Rosemary had managed to establish a clear direction for the integrated school and had introduced a distinct ethos that was based on inclusivity for all students, and engendered respect and responsibility at all times. This vision led immediately to a much more positive and pleasant learning environment for the whole school community. Enrolment increased markedly but there were limitations to the school's expansion, however well it performed, because it was housed in a wing of the old psychiatric hospital in Omagh. With its decaying plaster, obsolete heating, and a maze of corridors and hidden corners, much of the building was totally unsuitable for any modern school. Rosemary, along with parents and staff, pressed the politicians and relevant authorities for the funding to build a new school. Combined efforts finally paid off with ten and a half million allocated towards the building of new premises and in 2009 the students moved to a well-equipped modern school building.

One story of her time in the old school still gives us both a smile. A Christmas concert was underway and Rosemary had agreed to supervise the first year children as they waited in the wings for their turn to perform. Eleven-year-olds and their first concert is a recipe for excited chatter and Rosemary went backstage to calm them down.

'Sit down,' she whispered, 'like this,' and assumed the cross-legged lotus position. 'Now breathe in deeply and let out your breath with the "om" sound.' Rosemary demonstrated the technique to the rows of expectant faces. Things seemed to be going well when suddenly there was a tap on her shoulder. She turned round and a tiny girl stood behind her.

'Do you think you are in the right wing of this place, miss?'

A comedian in the making!

When she left the school, thanks to her success there, Rosemary was approached by the Westminster government to become a troubleshooter for schools in England that had problems and that required additional support or challenge. Sometimes this involved improving the ethos and behaviour of a school, or mentoring head teachers – on one occasion she was involved in amalgamating two large secondary schools into a single unit, and on another, converting a school into a new academy. In practice, this meant a very busy schedule of flying or driving to England for a few days each week and trying to catch up with house and garden at the weekends.

At that time, I had been asked by the Northern Ireland government to chair a task force on literacy and numeracy, and this too curtailed the amount of time that I could devote to the development of the garden. Before undertaking this work, like most people, I had always assumed Northern Ireland had a first-rate educational system. Unusually though, for any modern country, it is still strictly divided by religion, gender and ability. Nevertheless, at first glance, outcomes seem good and politicians and the media frequently make the comment that we have the best schooling in Europe. What a myth! The task force soon revealed, perhaps for the first time, that overall educational outcomes were very poor, with huge divisions between the most privileged students and those from disadvantaged backgrounds. On paper, the grammar schools achieved acceptable results – and so they should. If the schools select pupils (often privately coached) by ability, however suspect the test; provide them with cramming strategies to pass examinations; and discard those pupils who don't conform or who fall by the wayside, it is difficult not to appear successful. Though if a 'value added' calculation is considered (that is the additional learning students have achieved since they first entered the school) many are clearly underperforming.

Perhaps, though, the true test of any educational system is not how it deals with its brightest and most privileged children but how it deals with its less able or less fortunate. In this, the school system in Northern Ireland fails miserably. Annually there is a long tail of underachievement with many students leaving with few or no qualifications and too many failing schools with inadequate leaders. A recent Organisation for Economic Co-operation and Development (OECD) report put Protestant boys in Belfast second from the bottom of all European categories, one click above Roma children. Sadly this appalling situation still exists and it seems no one has the ability, interest or courage to take it on, but economically, socially and ethically it has to be acutely damaging to the country and the generations growing up in it. A sobering thought is that Northern Ireland now has more people with no qualifications than any other part of the UK.

One morning in 2004, during the first spring we spent in the house during the frog-breeding season, something quite exceptional happened. Rosemary was working in England and I had got up at first light to type up some of the recommendations for the literacy/numeracy report. I was sitting in the tower trying to get things in order but, as usual, was distracted by the scene in front of me. It was difficult to keep my mind on the manuscript and, looking out at the landscape, I noticed something disturbing the surface of the water in the middle pond. I focused the binoculars and watched. An otter! At first I could hardly believe what I was seeing – what an amazing privilege! Still in my dressing gown, I clattered downstairs, grabbed the camera, put on my wellies and set off for the lake. Every time the otter surfaced I stood stock-still and ran nearer each time it dived. Anyone watching me, clad only in dressing gown and green wellies with camera strung around my neck, first standing motionless and then sprinting like someone possessed, would have thought I had cracked, but finally I reached the observation shed without being spotted.

The otter emerged from behind the island and the automatic shutter on the Nikon rattled like a machine gun as he cruised across the surface not more than three metres away. I was entranced. The animal clearly had no idea I was there and I stared as it came out of the water and sat on the edge of the bank. I don't think I had realised just how big a fully grown otter looks when it's out of the water. Just when I was thinking that this spectacle couldn't get any better, I noticed a line of bubbles heading towards me across the surface. Another otter surfaced a few feet away, smaller this time, probably a female, and swam leisurely over to where the first one sat. I watched spellbound for ten minutes or so until suddenly they heard or scented something, dived and were gone.

Where they had come from we knew not, but it was the first of many sightings and we filmed them on the lawns, on the ice one winter when the lake froze over, and on one very special occasion when we saw an adult with two young. My most memorable encounter, though, came one day when I was sitting very still in the observation hut.

I was watching a pair of otters hunting in the lake, trying to get a few good pictures, when I sensed a movement to my left. The dog otter had climbed out of the water without me noticing and was now sitting a yard away, sniffing the air and watching me. Unfortunately the camera was down at my hip and I dared not move for fear of scaring him off so I pressed the shutter and hoped for the best. Though the resulting picture was slightly out of focus the experience of being so close to a wild creature was truly one to savour.

There was one phenomenon that occurred during the concentrated predation of the mating frogs by herons, otters and buzzards that I had never come across before. We kept finding jelly-like substances on the grass by the sides of the ponds. After a bit of research and asking around we discovered that it was usually called 'star jelly' or 'star shoot' and was at one time thought to have been caused by small meteorites falling to earth. The truth is much more mundane. Frogs' eggs are encased in a gelatinous substance. This frog jelly swells up greatly in volume by absorbing water and if a heron, or other bird, swallows a pregnant frog, it must vomit up the jelly. Hence the small mounds of translucent jelly found alongside ponds and water courses.

When the mating season had finished the frogs disappeared, followed by the buzzards and herons, and we were left to await the arrival of the tadpoles. Interestingly once they appeared, back came the herons to hunt them and the rainbow trout also joined the feast. Some anglers argue that these fish don't feed on tadpoles but those in our ponds certainly did. They came up from the depths, patrolled the margins of the lake and cruised around the edges until they came upon a concentrated cloud of tadpoles. Great swirls in the water would mark their attack and their intended victims would scatter in all directions. The food chain in action again.

★

In the meantime, as soon as the builders had left and human activity quietened down, we saw our first rabbit. We were expecting it because we had noticed a thriving population a mile or so away.

Rabbits were brought to the UK by the Normans in the twelfth century and, for nine hundred years following their introduction, they were seen as a really valuable asset because they bred rapidly, were a source of fur and provided a supply of much-needed protein during the winter months. Their flesh was tasty and easy to prepare, and a fully grown rabbit was just about the right size to be eaten at one meal so there was no waste. Initially the Normans kept them in walled enclosures called warrens, with specialist warreners in fortified houses alongside so they were on hand to fend off poachers. Some animals inevitably escaped or were purposely released from these compounds so by the 1700s the rabbit population in these islands had greatly expanded.

Changes to farming methods and the extensive planting of hawthorn hedges to enclose fields created an ideal habitat – colonies were able to develop burrows in the hedge bottoms right alongside their food supply. By the early twentieth century their numbers skyrocketed and farmers in many parts of the country regularly hired professional rabbit catchers to try to control rabbits and reduce the damage to crops. By 1950 it was estimated that the rabbits were inflicting an estimated fifty million pounds of damage to agriculture annually but when myxomatosis struck in 1953, 99 per cent of rabbits perished within two years.

Now the rabbit population is affected by Viral Haemorrhagic Disease (VHD) that impacts on them in autumn. The disease is highly contagious and seems to be endemic in this part of the world. It causes the blood of mature rabbits to clot. It is believed that rabbits are immune to this form of liver disease for the first two months of life so it can seem that populations are making a sustained comeback but then they fall back once the animals reach maturity. Populations do increase rapidly because the reproductive potential of the rabbit – a succession of litters of between three and seven young can be produced at intervals of thirty days throughout the summer. But in normal years the virus will take its toll in September and only the lucky few will survive. However some animals do seem to be developing a degree of immunity to the disease so we may be seeing the start of a revival.

Perhaps because of this disease, our first rabbit was sadly never seen again and it took another ten years before any others arrived to become permanent residents.

In terms of birdlife, we had no real idea about what species might be in the area so each new arrival was greeted with delight. Once our bird feeders, nesting boxes, plants with berries and new trees were in place, our first visitors in spring 2005, though largely predictable, were – for us in our green desert – really exciting. At the feeding station outside the kitchen window blue tits, coal tits, great tits, greenfinches, hedge sparrows, house sparrows, robins, goldfinches, siskins, collared doves and rooks appeared; seemed to like the peanuts, sunflower seeds, fat balls, old fruit and mixed grain on the menu; and became daily visitors.

The constant activity around the bird tables soon attracted the attention of sparrowhawks – one morning, a friend was looking out of the kitchen window watching the action on the feeders when the first attack occurred. A female bird, much larger than the male in this species, swooped in at high speed, its rounded wings and long rudder-like tail giving it a momentum and direction that is usually fatal for one of the birds gathered at any feeding table. On this occasion it hit a blackbird, knocked it to the ground in a cloud of feathers and mantled it whilst delivering the *coup de grâce*. The sparrowhawk left with the blackbird locked in its talons. It was all over in seconds and our visitor said in anger, 'I hate those things! They clear my bird table every few days. The small birds are terrified and won't come back for hours. I'm always finding remains of dead birds about and I wish something could be done to stop them.'

'Are you sure it's a sparrowhawk doing the damage?' I asked, knowing she kept several cats and lived in the centre of the town.

'Well, I've found half-eaten birds and their feathers.'

'Are they pulled out whole or sawn off near the base?'

'I've not looked. Why?'

'Sawn-off – cats or foxes; pulled out whole, like plucking a chicken, means hawks of some kind are responsible.'

'They wouldn't be my cats,' she said, to end the matter. 'It's definitely those murderous brutes.'

This oft-repeated opinion shows a misunderstanding of how well balanced the food chains are in successful wildlife gardens, and how interconnected the various elements have to be to keep all species happy. The toadstools tidy up the dead logs. The slugs and snails feed on the fungi. The thrush eats the slugs and snails before being taken by the sparrowhawk. It is a complex cycle to achieve equilibrium and interfering with any part of it can have serious consequences further down the line. Toxic chemicals and the industrialisation of the countryside increasingly skew that balance with devastating consequences for some species. So accepting that birds of prey and indeed all predators are a natural and necessary part of the jigsaw is surely more sensible than wishing that the events we occasionally observe and find uncomfortable don't happen.

The only predators I see differently are cats. They are an introduced species, and there are as many as ten million in these islands. They have few natural enemies, are allowed to roam wherever they like and, though some do not kill birds and small mammals, many do and the impact can be enormous. When we first started to develop the Fod and bird life began to multiply, we were plagued by dozens of semi-wild local farm cats. They would patrol the bird tables, often several at a time, and it was clear that if they were not removed they would severely hinder our long-term aspirations. Perhaps we have become far too tolerant of the predatory antics of these 'domestic tigers' and turn a blind eye to the damage they inflict of our native wildlife. Sparrowhawks kill to eat but cats kill for fun and I long to see a world where cats are kept in at night and where those that are wildlife-catching animals have to wear a bell on a quick-release collar. Not all cats hunt, of course, but it would be interesting to discover with some proper research just how much impact cats have on wildlife. In our case, the dog was always quick to scent any trespassing cats and would immediately give chase and run them off. The message seemed to get round and thankfully it is now rare to see a cat anywhere in the woods, meadows or garden. There are many cat lovers who would, of course, argue that their favourite tabby can do no wrong. This divided opinion is also true of one of our best-known native predators, the fox.

In 2006, for weeks on end, deep snow blanketed this part of Northern Ireland – the hardest winter we'd had since we moved in. A combination of low temperatures and sodden soil meant we lost many of our young shrubs, most of which we'd assumed were totally hardy. During this period, hunger forced the local fox population to become bolder. Roving animals were seen in broad daylight crossing country lanes, patrolling the perimeters of the pheasant-rearing pens in the forestry and foraging in domestic gardens. Telltale pad marks criss-crossed the frozen landscape and plentiful evidence of Reynard's exploits could be seen in remnants of carcasses, discarded wing feathers and the speedy disappearance of roadkill.

It was during this hard winter that we saw our first fox from the kitchen window. He was a magnificent dog fox, russet-coloured and in prime condition. He circled the bird table, picking up the odd titbit, before leisurely sauntering off towards the neighbour's henhouse. Seeing a truly wild creature like this – methodically quartering the ground, alert to every movement and sound, ever ready to pounce on any unwary victim – is surely one of the great wildlife sights of these islands. It is difficult not be moved by the curiosity, agility, efficiency and pure grace of this wild animal.

Of course there is another side to the fox, as everyone who has kept poultry will testify, and this has given him a different kind of reputation. As a ruthless, skilful and adaptable predator, the fox has few equals, which gets him into trouble whenever his natural hunting instinct clashes with human activity. He is a natural opportunist, and I suppose that this is the key characteristic that makes him hated by so many people. Make one mistake, leave the chickens' door open once, and he will spot the weakness and be in like a flash.

Foxes have not always been seen as the villains of the countryside. From the late eighteenth century, when fox hunting on horseback with packs of specially bred hounds began, wealthy landowners welcomed foxes. Whole new landscapes of small woodlands and coverts were created to encourage foxes to breed and to make the hunting of the open areas between these plantings more accessible for horses and riders. In fact there were often too few foxes to maintain good sport so artificial earths were constructed, and large numbers of captured animals were imported from the Continent, sold in markets and released. The landed gentry frowned upon the persecution or killing of these creatures except during a hunt, and shooting a fox was definitely not the done thing. Tensions arose when driven shooting grew in popularity in the late nineteenth and early twentieth century. Young pheasants can be protected to a certain extent but it is when the birds are strong enough to leave the pens but not sufficiently experienced to avoid the attentions of foxes that they are at their most vulnerable. Young pheasants and ducks will always draw in foxes from miles around.

Traditionally, in this part of Tyrone, farmers and gamekeepers have tried to reduce fox numbers by shooting or trapping but usually only with short-term success. Overall numbers in any one area vary little as the removal of local foxes merely creates a territorial vacuum that will soon be filled by new arrivals from the surrounding areas. Some will arrive from nearby farms where their numbers are not controlled but many undoubtedly move out from the adjacent towns, where urban foxes have multiplied in recent years. They have learnt to scavenge dustbins, rubbish tips and garden compost heaps, and seem quite at home breeding under potting sheds, on railway banks or in cemeteries. It is now not unusual to spot them crossing parks or roads at dusk or in the dark and, though they often look far less healthy than their country cousins, the foxes that have adapted to living in our towns are thriving and increasing in number. In built-up areas they are left largely undisturbed, have a guaranteed food supply and, apart from the danger of crossing busy roads, have few reasons not to multiply. Especially in July, when cubs are driven out by their parents and forced to seek new territories, semi-tame reared game birds and poultry must seem attractive.

For much of the year the diet of country foxes consists of slugs, frogs, carrion, roadkill, wild berries and – where they have made a comeback – rabbits. However, much as people hate to lose pheasants, duck or poultry to this ruthless predator, it is hard not to admire the resourcefulness, adaptability and sheer persistence of this intriguing animal. Although we may sometimes loathe what they do, our countryside would be much the poorer without them.

One of the neighbours we had when we lived in England would definitely not agree! One morning he looked utterly depressed as he stopped for a chat, 'A fox has been in during the night and had a ball with the chickens and ducks. It's my own fault,' he said. 'I went down to the pub to talk fishing with some of the boys. Got back late and forgot to shut them up. It's absolute carnage down there.'

Indeed it was. Feathers were everywhere. A number of headless fowl lay scattered across the orchard where the fox had cornered them and the survivors were perched high in the apple trees, still looking watchful and nervous. A trail of feathers led down into the bottom end of the orchard where brambles and blackthorn had created an overgrown corner.

'Looks like a fresh earth in there,' I said, pointing to what looked like new excavations. 'Must think he is in clover living this close to a chicken takeaway.'

The hole had that unmistakable acrid musk of fox and was clearly being used. Neat pad marks in the soft mud and the odd chicken feather confirmed that Reynard had indeed been in residence very recently. 'We'll give Foxy Fowler a call,' I said. 'He'll come over to sort you out.'

Foxy was the local terrier man. Every area has one. He loved ferreting and ratting but his real passion was going after foxes. Ask him to join a fox drive and he would be first there. Attending a meet of the hunt was something he never missed and being asked to sort out a troublesome fox was a request he could not refuse. His preferred method was simple, effective and brutal and I could never quite work out why he gained so much pleasure from it, but knew that once summoned he would be there within the hour.

His ancient Land Rover was soon at the farm and he jumped out amid a cloud of blue fumes, eager for the fray. He was small and wiry and quickly began to examine the remains in the orchard and the new diggings. He crawled on all fours to the entrance and put his head deep into the hole. He took a few deep breaths and announced dramatically, 'I think he's still in there. I'll get Rip.'

Rip was his secret weapon. A short-legged Jack Russell terrier that barked furiously in the back of the Land Rover in anticipation of the coming battle. It seems to me there are two types of Jack Russell terrier. Some are loving, affectionate dogs – totally trustworthy and wonderful companions. Others are like Rip – battled-hardened veterans that only the foolhardy would pet, that will fight anything without the slightest provocation and that have innately aggressive personalities.

I never once saw Foxy lock his Land Rover or remove the keys from the ignition, and when I asked him if this was sensible his response was to invite me to approach the vehicle. Rip appeared when I was still a yard away and put his mouth close to the glass. His gums were drawn back tight displaying piranha-like teeth and his eyes pinned me with a stare laced with malice. He was totally silent except for the sound of air being sucked through his clenched teeth but his message was crystal clear: 'Put your hand in here, son, and you will never play the piano again.'

I only once saw Rip and Foxy outmanoeuvred in the protection of their vehicle. We had gone to the car auctions in the city to make a bid on a Land Rover and parked in a back street, when two young lads came up. 'Look after your car for a pound, mister?'

'Rip does all the looking after I need,' said Foxy, pointing at the dog, who was already snarling at the boys.

'Does your dog put out fires?'

Foxy handed over his pound.

Rip was criss-crossed with scars from his many bloody encounters, and his hard, compact body trembled with excitement as Foxy carried him from the car towards the earth. He sniffed the hole, disappeared immediately and, within seconds, we could hear muffled but frantic barking from deep inside the earth. 'Rip's found him,' said Foxy. 'I'll get my spade.'

The spade was a family heirloom, its long handle polished from generations of use, and the narrow blade was worn, round and sharp. Foxy was proud of his inheritance and was fond of reminding everyone that the spade first belonged to his grandfather, was passed down to his father and until it finished up with him. 'This belonged to a professional rabbit catcher and is dead on for getting to ferrets that have killed underground, or earths on stony land or under tree roots. My father passed it on to me and he got it from his father. Our family have always hunted with this spade.' He slid his hand lovingly along the smooth shaft and began to dig.

It wasn't easy. The brambles and thorn had twined around buried machinery, broken tiles and other farmyard debris but Rip's incessant barking provided motivation and a narrow trench that followed the earth soon began to open up. As we got nearer, Rip's barking became even more frantic and Foxy leapt about, getting more excited by the minute. I was beginning to feel a little sorry for the fox, trapped at the end of a dark tunnel with dog and diggers getting ever closer, when Foxy suddenly reached his arm into the hole, grabbed the terrier and pulled him backwards. Rip hated being removed from the fray and bounced around trying to find a way past the spade that now blocked the hole.

'He's just behind my spade,' said Foxy. 'Pass me the Greener.' I loaded the single-barrel twelve-bore with full choke and brought it over to Foxy. It was at that moment that my neighbour, who had taken no part in the proceedings so far, stepped forward and said, 'I've never shot a fox. Do you mind if I have a go?'

Foxy looked a little doubtful but said, 'Shoot him when I move the spade away. You ready?'

'Yes,' came the reply.

'Now!' yelled Foxy. But the Greener roared prematurely. The spade was only part-way out before the shot chopped the shaft in half as cleanly as if it had been fed into a circular saw.

The narrow blade fell into the trench and rocked gently, as steam rose from the heat of the shot on the damp earth. Foxy fell back still holding the shattered remains of his spade. 'Feck,' he said.

'Whoops! Sorry about that! Got a bit overexcited there,' said the farmer.

The fox peeked out, saw its chance for freedom, bolted and was gone in a second.

'Feck,' said Foxy again. He picked up the remnants of his beloved spade and ambled away to his Land Rover, the muddy terrier under his arm. The Land Rover coughed into life and the cloud of blue fumes hid Foxy from view.

'Feck' we heard again as his vehicle disappeared down the lane.

It would have been anathema to Foxy but we were always, at least in the early days before we had poultry, pleased to see foxes patrolling the garden and looking quite at home in the new environment. Most days we spotted something new to confirm the theory that if wildlife is in the area and like what they find they will come.

An unexpected benefit of this kind of wildlife gardening was the discovery of lines of wood blewits. We had picked these delicious edible fungi, with their purple-tinged gills and buffish tops many times around our home in Sherwood Forest but thought wrongly, as it turned out, that they only grew in sandy country. Plenty of them appeared in autumn under the deciduous trees we had planted but how long their spores had lain dormant in the soil before the woodland came we had no idea. It was certainly a puzzle that we hoped to investigate further, but in the meantime we decided that, accompanied by sausage, bacon, black pudding, a free-range egg, Irish potato bread and a pot of tea, they would undoubtedly make a gourmet treat to savour!

7

More Newcomers

Anyone who has started a garden from scratch, especially on wet, rough land, will know how slow progress can seem. Our friend Jim, the forestry man, had given us some advice about the trees that cheered us up: 'Plant them, then forget about them for the first three years. Once the roots are down you will see them start to motor.' He was absolutely right and by 2008, the fifth year after we started, it was clear that the hedges, small spinneys and shrubberies were really beginning to thicken up.

Around the time we bought the site, Rosemary gave me a new camera for my birthday, so we were able to take pictures of everything from day one. We took shots of hedge planting, lake digging, tree planting and building and soon had a comprehensive pictorial record of the whole project, including pictures of any bird, butterfly or animal that appeared. This collection of images was useful because it was a reminder both of how far we had come and how inhospitable and uninviting the original site had been. In fact, looking back, we often thought we were quite mad to start on something like this in the first place but were soon reassured when we compared current pictures with earlier images.

The interest in photography got me into a comical encounter on one occasion. We had gone down to the coast in Donegal for the day and had walked for miles along Murvagh beach. It was late by the time we were coming home so we thought we'd try an award-winning fish and chip shop in Omagh. As I was waiting for our cod and chips the local press photographer walked in. We had met a few times on civic or educational occasions and I began the conversation by saying, 'Rosemary bought me a super camera, a Nikon D300, but getting the white balance exactly right is not easy. Do you have any suggestions?'

'No. I'm not too familiar with that kind of camera. Is it digital?'

'Yes,' I said, very puzzled. 'I load the pictures up to my computer and then edit them in Photoshop, but the technology isn't easy to understand at first. Do you use something like that in your work?'

'No. I'm not into computers – it's still only old-fashioned, traditional techniques with me.'

I was astounded. A modern press photographer not using digital or electronic editing. The food arrived, I said goodbye but was still chuntering to myself when I got back into the car.

'What are you muttering about?' Rosemary asked.

'The press photographer in there – he knows absolutely nothing about modern cameras or computers!'

With that, the 'photographer' walked out of the chippy and waved.

'You know why?' she said, smiling. 'It's because he's the local cobbler.'

Weeks later, when I met the real photographer, he roared with laughter at the story and invited me round to the studio to give me some shortcuts for the camera and some tips about editing. Strangely, the cobbler still avoids me!

Walking around the boundaries on all of our new internal paths was a great way of checking progress. We carried out this ritual in hail, rain or shine every day. It wasn't just that we were both slightly obsessive about noting the progress of the garden, but we now had two dogs that needed daily exercise. Sal, the black Labrador we had brought from England, finally died aged sixteen. Losing an old dog is never easy and we knew the search to find her successor would be difficult because breeding, intelligence, size and appearance are all vital qualities in a working Labrador. We toured most of Northern Ireland looking at dogs for sale before being attracted by a particular puppy that was seven months old. When we arrived at the kennels, the breeder explained he had five dogs and was selling them all to start a business. The puppy looked perfect. Great pedigree, right size, lively. The decision to buy him was instant but then the owner surprised us when he announced that the mother was part-trained and if we bought her we could have the puppy at a reduced price. The bitch also looked an excellent dog but at that stage we had not considered getting two so we hesitated. After a pause he said that if we bought the mother we could have the puppy at no cost. This was a bargain too good to miss, especially given that the dogs were so well bred, so we shook hands and sealed the deal.

On the way home we telephoned our three sons to pass on the news of the purchases and to ask for suggestions for a name for the new dog. We didn't really need to ask, as it turned out, as they all suggested the name that we already had in mind – Boatswain, shortened eventually to Bosie. Why did we all think of the same name? In Nottinghamshire we lived a few miles from Newstead Abbey, home of Lord Byron and the famous monument to his favourite dog – Boatswain!

By 2008, as the habitat matured, new arrivals came thick and fast. Mistle thrushes, redwings and fieldfares, all members of the thrush family, appeared in droves once the winter weather hit – the rowan, holly, hawthorn and cotoneaster berries were stripped in days. Charms of goldfinches swirled over the thistles and seed heads in the meadow; mallard, teal, moorhens and reed buntings discovered the ponds. Rare passers-by sometimes dropped in. An odd, eel-like, red-breasted merganser one morning; a cormorant sitting on the observations hut; a tiny dabchick; and on several occasions a charming merlin – apart from the bird of prey, these were species that we didn't even know were in the area.

Happily neighbours, who previously had little interest in wildlife, heard about what we were trying to do and many got fully behind the project. They installed bird feeders in their gardens and it was soon apparent that this chain of feeding stations was leading to substantial increases in small bird populations. Greenfinches and goldfinches especially seemed to benefit from the change of habitat on our land.

We got to know the regular inhabitants of the plot well and as we had our tea and toast each morning and surveyed the scene, it felt like being in a habitat soap opera.

'The long–tailed tits and family have moved out.'

'There's a pair of ravens passing. They're nesting in those pines on the edge of the forest.'

'Not many duck about this morning – they must still be feeding on those barley stubbles.'

Most mornings there was something moving about, feeding, crossing the patch or watching. Rosemary summed it up perfectly one morning when she said, 'There is now activity everywhere my eye settles. Finally this looks like the garden we had in Sherwood Forest.'

We were astonished by how much it had all changed. The dream we had, that had certainly looked doubtful at times, was beginning to come together!

In the early days we were unsure of how much natural food was available, so decided to supplement things by providing artificial feeders. We placed a hopper with wheat in the meadow and distributed barley round the shallow margins of the lakes. Parties of teal and mallard soon spotted this food source and would arrive each evening to feed. Shooters hunted them on the local rivers so the birds were always wary and alert. As soon as we appeared they were instantly airborne and heading off, and it seemed a pity we could not get them to stay on the ponds during the day. We tried introducing a few reared duck and some call ducks but they soon disappeared, or were caught by the otters or foxes. In the end we accepted that the visiting ducks were truly wild birds and if we wanted to watch them it would only be at dawn or dusk.

However things changed in 2010 when our friend Gillian arrived from Fintona with four mallard in a cardboard box. The ducklings had been left behind by their mother. Gillian's husband, Richard, had rescued them from a cat and had managed to rear them in his barn and now asked if he could release them on our pond. Of course we agreed and three drakes and one duck swam round, flew a couple of circuits and finally settled back in to feed. The Fintona Four have stayed ever since. They leave in the mornings with the other wildfowl but usually return during the day, so their presence is a welcome compromise – mallard that are wary enough to stay safe but trusting enough not to leave the minute they spot us.

Duck have bred annually on our ponds and numbers in the vicinity have increased markedly since we began the wildlife project. Seeing newly hatched ducklings is always pure joy and watching their antics always reminds me of one of the most extraordinary students I ever taught.

I worked in a tough secondary school in a mining area and was in my office one day when the internal telephone rang. It was Joe from the main office, who – via the monitor – had seen a boy cross the quadrangle and begin to climb the drainpipe to the roof of the library. In a few seconds he had shinned up to the stone lintels on the top of the parapet, hauled himself over and disappeared from view.

Joe added, 'He's just climbing on to the roof of your block.

Didn't recognise him – must be a first year boy. Went up that downpipe outside Room Eight like a monkey.'

'Okay, Joe. I'll sort it.'

The library was a modern extension to a traditional school building which had existed on the site for fifty or so years. It was designed to house computers and a recording studio as well as books. Its modern furniture and the floor-to-ceiling windows created a sharp contrast to the gloomy classrooms along the adjoining corridors. It was single storey and the low pyramidal shaped roof had been planted with mosses and lichens to form a green area that the architects had promised would be more efficient and eco-friendly. A yard-high perimeter wall, cloaked on the inside with asphalt and tar, enclosed the whole area. It was into the concealed part that the pupil had climbed.

A window at the back of the English department storeroom gave a view along the length of the roof so I peered through. As well as the moss-covered section, the roof had an assortment of skylights; two small huts to house aerials and electrical sub stations; and a water tank. Everything was as normal and at first I could see no one. Then a movement caught my eye and a small boy moved stealthily out from behind a ventilator cover and came forward into view. He held a long-handled net out in front of him and was clearly stalking something in the corner of the parapet, for he suddenly lunged and then crouched down to examine whatever it was that now appeared to be trapped in the mesh. I quietly unlocked the access door, stepped out on to the roof and made my way across to the corner where he was sitting. He held something in cupped hands and was so engrossed in examining his catch that he did not hear my approach. I recognised him as a first year pupil from one of my classes who was always courteous, curious about everything and very likeable.

'Brian, what on earth are you doing up here?' I asked in my sternest teacher voice.

He looked up, seemingly unperturbed, and said, 'Hello, sir.

Have you come to help?'

'Help what?'

'To catch these ducklings,' and he held out the tiny, fluffy, yellow-and-brown bird now peeping out from his lightly clenched fist. 'There are more over there,' he added, pointing to the corner of the mossy roof where several other tiny birds buzzed around like angry wasps. He lifted the flap of a cardboard box at his side and gently placed the captured duckling into it before saying, 'If you walk them round, sir, I'll try and get them into the net.'

'Hold on, Brian. Please explain things to me.' I sat down on the roof to listen to what he had to say.

'A few weeks ago I was standing in the playground and saw a female mallard land up here on the roof. I thought it unusual but it seemed to come from the eco-pond down by the science lab and I wondered what was going on. When I was taking the readers back to the storeroom from English I looked out of the window and saw that the duck had built a nest in the moss on the roof. She wasn't sitting but was coming each day to add another egg to the clutch. The bird had chosen a safe place for a nest but the more I thought about it, the more worried I got about how she was going to get the ducklings down from the roof once they hatched. The wall on the edge is too steep.'

Unwittingly, perhaps because of the boy's obvious enthusiasm and commitment to the preservation of the ducklings, I had somehow been drawn in to this enterprise as a willing accomplice. Instead of staying in teacher mode and challenging him about the crazy idea of climbing up a drainpipe to reach a roof, I found myself asking him with some incredulity, 'How did you know they would hatch today?'

'Once all the eggs were laid and she started sitting I knew it would take about twenty-eight days and I had a note in the diary for today or tomorrow. I saw the duck and nine ducklings from the storeroom window this morning when I fetched the readers.'

'How many have you caught so far?'

'Six. Three more are over by the corner.'

'Where is the adult duck?'

'She took off when I got here but she won't be far away, and she'll gather up the ducklings once we get them down.'

We soon gathered the last of the brood and placed them in the box and carried them (via the safe storeroom route) down to ground level. We gently released them on to the edge of the school pond and, as Brian had predicted, the adult mallard was quickly in attendance and led the family into the reed beds and out of sight.

'I applaud your compassion and initiative, Brian, but in future come and ask me about things like this. Climbing that drainpipe was a very dangerous stunt and could have ended in serious injury. Don't ever do anything like that again! Understand?'

'Yes, sir. Sorry, sir,' and with that he was gone, diary in hand.

I came to know that Brian was a boy fascinated by wildlife of every kind. At such a young age his knowledge of birds, mammals and insects was impressive, and in the evenings or at weekends he would roam every inch of the local countryside to update the records in what he called his naturalist's diary. Some of his classmates clearly saw him as slightly eccentric but it did not seem to bother Brian in the slightest – he appeared quite proud of his nickname Birdy. He came from a mining family and lived in one of the dismal terraces that were hastily constructed alongside the new collieries to house the influx of miners from Scotland, Wales and coalfields across England. The estates had been slapped into the heart of pristine countryside near the pit and were now surrounded by a sprawl of buildings, railway sidings, shops and pubs.

A few months later I was walking along the corridor and came face to face with Brian.

'Is it all right if I ask you something, sir?'

'No problem, as long as doesn't involve scaling roofs after ducks.'

First to arrive were the frogs.

Then came the wild duck.

Otters appeared – this one watching me!

Moorhens nested.

Unusual visitors like the cormorant turned up.

Sparrowhawks became regulars.

House martins used mud from the lake for nest building.

And Boatswain used the lake for exercise.

Pheasants soon appeared . . .

. . . and made themselves at home!

Rabbits came to stay . . .

. . . and the first Irish hares seen in these parts for thirty years arrived.

Wood pigeon numbers have increased as farmers move
from pasture to grain.

Wrens are among the sixty-four species of bird we have
recorded on the Fod.

We have spotted twelve species of mammal so far,
including grey squirrels and mice.

'Wrong season, sir,' he said with a grin.

'Yes. Of course. Fire away.'

'Well, I was watching a programme on TV last night called *All Creatures Great and Small* and I thought that when I leave school I would like to be a vet but I don't know what to do to get a job like that so I thought I would ask you.'

I was chasing up some pointless admin which needed completing and almost asked him to come to see me later, but he looked so eager and expectant that I instead asked if he had a sheet of paper I could use.

Few if any of the people in Brian's neighbourhood had been to university and most saw an apprenticeship at the colliery as the natural step after leaving school. I knew his dream of a career with animals might prove a tall order. On the other hand he was very intelligent and, as the mallard-on-the-roof incident had proved, could be incredibly purposeful when he had a clear goal in mind.

So I took the paper and, speaking as I wrote, started with the title 'To be a Vet' and went carefully through the list of requirements. 'First, you will have to get seven or eight very good grades in your fifth-year GCSE examinations. Showing an affinity with animals will also help so working at the kennels, pet shop, local vet's surgery, farms, the donkey sanctuary and anything else you can think of will support your case. Ask Mr Townsend for addresses, contacts and telephone numbers – he has them all on file. Three or four A levels – Biology, Chemistry, Physics and Maths would be ideal, and you will have to get straight As. That may seem tough but getting there will be very competitive. Then you will have to apply to vet school – the Royal Veterinary College in London is a good one – and the course will last five or six years depending on the options you take. That's about it.' At the end of the list I wrote in capital letters 'and THEN YOU'LL BE A VET OK!'

'Thanks, sir,' he said, carefully folding the sheet and putting it into his blazer pocket before disappearing at pace down the corridor.

Brian became an excellent scholar and seemed to sail effortlessly through his studies whatever the subject. Nine top grades at GCSE were predicted and achieved and at weekends and evenings he systematically built up a network of contacts with all the animal charities, shops and surgeries that I had suggested. He signed up for four A levels and, in addition, registered at the local further education college to duplicate his course in physics because he didn't rate the teacher at school. An opinion with which I have to say I agreed.

Towards the end of his first term in the sixth form he came along to see me. 'Do you mind if I ask your advice, sir?'

'Course not. Have you discovered bats in the bell tower?'

'No such luck, sir. No, I have a problem at home.'

Over a cup of tea he explained that his father thought that Brian staying at school for another two years was going to be a bit of a struggle for the family, and that spending more years at university would certainly be a bridge too far. His father knew that, after basic training and working weekends, it would be possible for Brian to earn five or six hundred pounds a week at the pit – which was more than the teachers at school were paid – so his father felt that a job at the colliery was the best option.

Brian looked thoroughly downcast and I asked, 'Is your father set on this idea?'

'I think so, sir.'

'What about Mum?'

'Not so keen but she usually goes along with what Dad wants.'

'Will it help if I chat to them?'

'That's what I was hoping because you might be able to put forward another view. Dad won't come up to school, though. He hated the experience he had here and, though I've told him times have changed, he still has a poor opinion of teachers and says he'll never set foot in this place again.'

'Could we meet at your house?'

'I'll ask'.

'Try and arrange it and I'll come down.'

We met a few evenings later and I listened without comment while Brian's dad delivered a long tirade about the brutal treatment and poor teaching he had experienced during his time at school. The injustice of this time clearly still rankled with him and the wounds remained raw.

Eventually his wife intervened and asked, 'Do you think Brian should look for a job at the colliery?'

'Well, he is a very bright student with tremendous potential and ...'

'Nothing wrong with going down the pit,' Dad cut in. 'Plenty of coal still left and seams are wide and easy to get at so the mine here has a safe future. With overtime he can earn a good living. So in my view, that's that.'

His argument seemed to be mainly about money so I took a gamble. 'How much do you earn at the pit?'

'That's my business.'

I turned to his wife and asked cheerily, 'How much does he earn?'

'I'm not saying,' she laughed.

'Well I've printed out some likely salaries someone of Brian's ability could expect once he graduates. Perhaps you might like to take a look at them later on.'

Those which might be earned by vets in private practice were last on the list and, I have to admit, were slightly exaggerated, but I passed the sheet over, thanked them for their hospitality, got up and left.

Next morning Brian was at my office first thing with a spring in his step. 'Worked, sir! Dad left me a note this morning saying that I should apply and see if I can get into vet school.'

'That's great, Brian. Let me take a look at your application and personal statement before you send it and we'll keep fingers crossed.'

Predictably his completed forms were near perfect and his statement showed a passion for studying veterinary science that leapt out from the page. His history, achievements to date and potential grades were impressive so a few weeks later I was stunned when he informed me that his application to London had been turned down. No reasons were given and I felt so aggrieved that I phoned the university admissions officer to seek an explanation. He was evasive and very complacent, telling me that it wasn't university policy to give out specific information on individual students and that the selection procedures were carried out fairly. However he would not tell me what these procedures were and why some candidates were rejected. I went through everything that Brian had undertaken in order to make himself such a strong candidate.

I seemed to be getting nowhere so in exasperation I finally asked, 'Has anyone actually read his application or has he simply been dismissed because of the kind of school he comes from?'

That finally did seem to get under his skin and I think more to get rid of me than due to any compassion for Brian's case he finally said, 'I'll get someone to take another look to see if we have missed something,' and put the phone down.

The letter to Brian was curt and informed him that his application had been 'reappraised' and he had a provisional place at the university depending on achieving his predicted grades. Should he be successful, his performance would be reviewed at the end of the first year.

Off he went to London. Five or six years later, Brian's mum rang to give us the news that he had just qualified as a vet, came out second-highest student in the whole of the college, had been offered a part-time post as lecturer at the university and had landed a plum job in private practice. They were having a few beers and sandwiches at the local miners' welfare at the weekend to celebrate and Brian had asked specifically if we could attend.

As Rosemary and I walked in, he immediately came across to us through the crowd. He looked very mature, confident and self-assured.

'Brian, we are both delighted you finally cracked it!' I said. 'No one deserves this success more than you do. Well done!'

'Thanks, sir,' he said. 'I have to admit that I am pretty pleased. Oh, and by the way, here's your paper back,' he smiled, handing me a well worn, folded sheet.

I opened it up and it was the page of advice I had given him on how to become a vet. He had ticked off every item on the list and where I had written, 'and THEN YOU'LL BE A VET OK!' he had added, 'I am a vet – OK!' Memories of that moment still bring a lump to my throat.

Although the Fintona Four seem to have settled happily with us there have also been disappointments. We haven't spotted the barn owl recently, for example, and no one else has seen it either, even though in the early days we often used to see one on the bales in the stubble fields and, once, on the rafters in one of the barns. Agriculture in our immediate area changed slightly a few years ago as rising cereal prices and falling cattle prices tempted many farmers to plough up existing pastureland and plant barley or wheat. This trend accelerated and fields of ripening corn now dominate, where once there was a more traditional landscape of grassland and cattle. Obviously small rodents are attracted to barley and wheat fields and our hope is that any barn owls resident in the region have followed their prey and now frequent these new habitats.

Similarly we have not seen the water rails since those early days. They may still be there, but hidden by the now-thickened reed beds. They are always very elusive but it could also be that they have fallen prey to herons or just moved on. We still hear the odd one but not in the concentrated way of those early days, and we have certainly never seen any more water rail chicks. We live in hope!

To begin with, we regularly heard the distinctive sound of the male cuckoos once they arrived in April and occasionally spotted them in flight as they crossed the front of the tower. Unfortunately their numbers suddenly declined and by 2017 we were only spotting the odd one. This sadly is also the case with the curlew. They used to come regularly to the boglands alongside our garden, but suddenly the visits stopped and we have not seen one for some time. Their decline cannot be linked to changes in the habitat in this part of Ireland because the bogland in our locality remains as it has been for hundreds of years and, apart from the snipe shooters later in the year and the brief attempts to create a tip, any disturbance of their breeding grounds has been minimal. It seems more likely that the causes of their sudden disappearance must be found beyond our shores.

The change from pasture to cereal growing is a good illustration of how changes in habitat can quickly impact on wildlife patterns. When we first came to Tyrone and began to develop the garden, spotting a wood pigeon was a very rare event. I spent my youth in rich farming country. Wheat dominated the landscape, with barley, potatoes and oilseed rape used for crop rotation. Huge numbers of wood pigeon thrived on this cereal diet and, in the winter, old potato fields or the green leaves of the rape ensured that many of the birds survived even the hardest weather. In Nottinghamshire we were used to seeing huge concentrations of the birds, especially at harvest time, so the absence of pigeon in our part of Ireland was quite striking. I had wondered if the change in the land use might benefit the wood pigeon population – and it has. They are now much more numerous, nesting annually in the hedgerows. We see them most mornings and evenings, moving between their roost sites and the feeding grounds.

Recently we tried taking advantage of new technology by installing a hidden trail camera near the lake to see if water rails were still about. No rails appeared but the camera was excellent at showing the range of species which appear when we are not around. For the first time we saw hedgehogs, grey squirrels and the odd rat, and were amazed by the number of jays and pheasants that appeared.

We had of course seen pheasants in the garden many times – they were reared and released by gamekeepers in the nearby Seskinore Forest – but we never saw chicks or found nests. It is argued that reared birds do not nest easily in the wild and that, in this country, there are too many predators for the sitting birds to survive. As the habitat developed and safe nesting cover became available the assumption that the land would never support the breeding of wild game birds proved to be false. We first saw a clutch of newly hatched pheasants in the meadow and watched over the next few weeks as they grew into poults and finally became mature birds. Some of their number fell by the wayside, either through disease or predation, but enough survived to show that, given a habitat which suited both adult birds and chicks, pheasants would breed successfully. Later in the year nests and the remains of hatched eggs were found in the meadow to confirm that the chicks had in fact originated from our land.

The local gamekeepers stop feeding the birds at the end of the shooting season and we wondered what would happen if we bought a couple of standard game feeders and kept them filled with grain for the whole year. The two plastic bins, with a spring arrangement at the bottom which allows the pheasants to reach up and shake a few grains at a time from the base, were placed in the meadow and in a corner near one of the lakes. Numbers seen in the garden immediately increased and several of these went on to breed successfully. What surprised us somewhat were the numbers involved – we'd sometimes see as many as twenty at a time, and it is now very rare to walk around the woods and lakes without coming across these birds.

Pheasant rearing for sport was, of course, big business on the large estates in the past and many landowners still release large numbers of birds each year. In the past, formal driven shooting of pheasants was only available to the aristocracy, extremely wealthy or the very well connected. This form of the sport reached its peak in the Edwardian era when, on one estate, 3,937 pheasants were shot in a single day. Even in those days the cost of artificially boosting pheasant numbers was astronomical and maintaining a shoot bankrupted several landowning families. The old cynical saying of 'up goes a guinea, bang goes a penny-halfpenny and down comes half a crown' still rings true today as shoots wrestle with rising costs. Today two to three hundred birds a day are shot on the biggest driven shoots and at a cost of £37 per bird, it is still the pursuit of the very wealthy! Not everyone will agree with rearing birds for sport of course but I'm sure that many country residents are, like us, glad to have the refugee pheasants as additions to their gardens' birdlife.

On one occasion we spotted one red-legged partridge but we have never seen a native grey partridge and it is unlikely that we ever will. It is now agreed that at some time in the 1980s this native bird became extinct in Northern Ireland. Few people seemed to be aware of its decline and it slipped away with barely a whimper of protest from farmers, conservationists, wildlife enthusiasts or sportsmen. Sadly the species is also disappearing across most of Europe and it has long been known that the decline in the UK and Ireland over the last fifty years has been due to changing agricultural practices. Extensive research identified the widespread use of agrochemicals as the principal factor behind this decline, along with the introduction of modern silage-cutting machines. Herbicides killed off the arable weeds, which supported insect life such as sawfly larvae, a vital food source for the newly hatched chicks. Fast-moving mowers, cutting the pastures at the height of the breeding season, destroyed both nests and sitting birds. The result was an 80 per cent decline in grey partridge numbers in England and Wales, and almost total extinction in Ireland. Many argue that the widespread rearing of pheasants also has an impact in that they carry a parasite that, though harmless to the host, is very damaging to the smaller game bird. All this doesn't stop us dreaming that one day, if the habitat is right, we'll hear the evocative call of the grey partridge coming from our meadow at dawn and dusk.

Although our meadow still doesn't look anything like the ones in the gardening books, it began to attract an impressive array of butterflies, moths, bees and other insects. We saw meadow browns in large numbers, followed at intervals by cabbage white, tortoiseshell, peacocks, orange tip, red admirals and painted ladies. Quite a pleasing list, given that a few years earlier it would have been rare to see a single one on the land.

One summer evening Catherine, aka the butterfly lady, came from Butterfly Conservation to set up moth traps in the meadow. We had met one evening when I was speaking to a gardening club and she suggested it might be interesting to come over and survey our site to see what was about. She wasn't at all surprised by what she found but we were astonished: there was a huge range of species and an enormous number of moths flitting around our garden after dark. There were those we recognised such as emperors, hawk moths, cinnabar and the garden tiger, but the majority we had never seen before. Catherine kindly identified them including some of the tiny micro moths. We realised once more that we were truly beginners in this wildlife game.

On one occasion we created a perfect habitat by accident. The severe winter of 2010 had devastated the number of wrens in the garden but their recovery in subsequent years was assisted greatly by one of our mistakes. We had put up a greenhouse as part of the courtyard at the rear of the house and, though we built a window on one side, we neglected to fit a roof window so it was impossible to ventilate the apex. All manner of insects were trapped there either by spiders' webs or by the rising heat. Wrens soon spotted this concentration of dead or dying insects and would slip in through the open door or window to scoop up this windfall. During the breeding season, especially when adults were feeding their young, there were often six wrens using this impromptu feeding station. Needless to say, the wren population in the garden is now very healthy.

Ever since the first season following the building of the courtyard and the open-sided shed, swallows have arrived and have nested there. Spotting the first swallow twisting overhead always lifts my heart and, whatever the date, this bird heralds the start of spring for me. At least two broods are reared to each pair and it is truly delightful to sit and watch the parents flying endless circles before swooping down once more to fill the gaping mouths of their chicks. Juveniles from earlier hatches often assist in the feeding of the next generation. It is always wonderful to remember that these birds, young and old, will gather at the end of the season and complete a journey of thousands of miles to return to South Africa.

So far the swift boxes have only been home to families of sparrows and starlings – no swifts – but at least this means they have not been entirely wasted. We have seen the occasional swift flying high over the land, and they do nest in the village four miles away, so perhaps they will find us some day. But the wide eaves on the house have proved highly suitable for the visiting house martins. In the second season, eleven pairs decided this would make an ideal habitat and began to collect the tiny mud pellets from the lake sides. Up to 2,500 specks of mud are required to build the nest of concentric bands. It is staggering to realise that these tiny birds can construct this dome, line it with feathers and begin the process of breeding in such record time. Interestingly, the artificial nests we purchased at great expense and mounted under the eaves have never been used. It is difficult to understand why but perhaps they need even more time to weather before the birds will take an interest.

One fine summer evening we were sitting with guests in the courtyard at the rear of the house and the martins and swallows were in constant attendance. Three pairs of swallows were feeding young inside the covered area and were constantly swooping low over our heads to get to the hungry broods. The house martins were also there in number, tracking backwards and forwards, not much above head height.

One of the guests seemed to duck involuntarily each time the birds skimmed by and finally said, 'I know you two promote wildlife but I couldn't be doing with these birds about all of the time. They unnerve me.'

I explained about migration and the life cycle of these fascinating birds in the hope it might be possible to change minds but it seemed a lost cause.

Later on in the evening the same person said, 'We can't sit out in our garden at this time of the evening because we get bitten by midges.'

'What you need are some of these little friends to help you out,' I replied, pointing at the swallows and martins and smiling.

We love the day when the house martin chicks leave the nests and take their first flight. Dozens of fresh birds appear to join our local residents and for a few hours a joyous aerial party takes place with young and old diving and soaring with obvious pleasure. At the end of each summer, when the martins and swallows finally return to Africa, the garden feels strangely empty and still.

Photographing and watching wildlife had always been a bit of an obsession for me but as the garden matured and more species arrived, creating a photographic record became part of my daily routine. I would put on boots and weatherproofs, release the dogs and set off with my camera round my neck to see what was about.

These amblings could take well over an hour and, with much sitting and waiting, could often be much longer. I would sit still and observe the comings and goings, but getting close without building elaborate hides was always difficult. I thought a new purchase offered a solution – a full sniper camouflage suit. It had enormously wide trousers that covered my boots and a jacket with mittens attached, and all parts were covered in dozens of strips of camouflage material sewn on to the base cloth. To complete the outfit, there was a hood, also draped with lengths of camo, to zip around the neck. It was huge and heavy, and it looked like moving around in it would be cumbersome, hot and slow. Only my eyes would be visible when the hood was zipped on. That was perhaps no bad thing, because donning it would certainly make the wearer seem slightly mad, a cross between a compost heap and a walking bush. Perhaps the only saving grace was that, once inside it, I would be completely unrecognisable to the outside world.

Some sika deer had been seen at a farm over the hill and I had driven over to see if I could get a few good pictures. This seemed the ideal opportunity to try out my new suit. I parked near the farm gate, and got out of the car as discreetly as possible, ducking down out of sight whenever other cars passed. After struggling into the suit, I zipped up the hood as quickly as possible, took the camera out of its case and lumbered off out of public gaze towards the distant hillside where I hoped to get some pictures. Walking was hard. The suit rubbed and rustled and, though I was only wearing boxer shorts and a vest underneath, I was soon overheating as I waddled along like a deep-sea diver. Finally, I reached a good vantage point on the edge of the wood, sat down and instantly became part of the landscape. Within minutes, the local wildlife became active and seemed to ignore my presence. A grey squirrel came within a few feet of me. Several wood pigeon flew in to an overhead ash. It was as if I didn't exist. The signs looked good – I decided to test the suit in open country and shuffled out into the centre of the meadow to lie down. In no time rabbits emerged from their burrows. I lined up the camera very gingerly, focused on the nearest rabbit and pressed the shutter in the hope of getting a good range of shots. Brilliant suit, I thought, tremendous potential, and I settled down to wait for the deer.

The morning turned into one of those warm spring days when it feels winter is truly over and I lay listening to the sounds of the countryside. I heard a rare yellowhammer in the hedgerow, collared doves mewed nearby and the unmistakable croak of a raven came on the breeze from somewhere in the distance. It was one of those times when it is a joy to be alive and I dozed as I lay there.

I awoke with a start. Heavy drops of rain were falling on my back and the rattle of machinery seemed very close. I scrambled to my feet and realised with horror that during my snooze a tractor spreading slurry had entered the field and was spurting an arc of foul-smelling liquid across the pasture. It was this that was pattering down on my new suit. I shuffled off towards the sanctuary of the nearby wood as fast as I was able and, as I fled, I noticed that the tractor had stopped and the driver was out of his cab staring transfixed in my direction. I am sure he had no understanding of what he was seeing – this sighting would probably become the start of a new Bigfoot legend in these parts.

Some slurry had definitely dotted the camo strips on my back and the stink followed me all the way back to the car. I opened the boot, put the camera back in its case and began to unzip the hood from the body of the suit – but in my haste to fasten the hood, I had caught the strips in the teeth of the zip. For a good few minutes, I tugged, pulled and cursed but the fastener just would not move. I realised I would have to drive home with the hood on and slammed the boot down in frustration.

Do you ever do something which a second later you wish you hadn't? My car has an electronic fob that opens the car and the boot separately. I had opened the boot to put the camera back in, leaving the keys sitting on top of the Nikon bag. I was well and truly locked out, festooned from head to foot in stinking camouflage strips. There was a spare key back at the house but my money and phone were in the car. I couldn't take off the whole suit as the day was cold and I only had boxer shorts and vest underneath, so it dawned on me that I had no alternative but to walk the four miles home.

The first part of the trek was along tiny country lanes and fortunately no vehicles came along, but the main road was entirely different. I tried hitching a lift but standing alongside the hedgerow, no cars stopped. I suppose they didn't actually see me. A few honked their horns, and someone in a works van yelled a friendly greeting of 'pervert' as they passed. I weathered this unwanted attention, and shuffled along safe in the knowledge that at least no one knew who was concealed beneath the costume. Further along the road an elderly lady stood at the gate of her bungalow. The small white terrier at her side growled softly as I ambled up.

'Shut up, Toby!' she said, and then addressed me. 'Not a bad day. Bit on the cold side but not a bad day. Smells like someone's spreading slurry.'

'Great to see a dry day after all the rain we've had,' I replied, my voice sounding muffled from inside the hood.

'Not from round here are you?'

'No,' I said, amazed she had made absolutely no reference to my absurd-looking suit, and the fact that she could only see my eyes.

'Thought so. Foreigner?'

'No. I'm just heading home. I live near Seskinore Forest.' What a stupid thing to say when you are dressed from head to toe as a tree, but she made no comment.

'Had a cousin lived in Seskinore,' she muttered. 'We had to put her in a home.'

'Well I'd best be on my way. Good to meet you,' I said,

preparing to move off.

'Is someone looking after you?' she said. I shook my head and said nothing. The white terrier was cocking its leg on my trousers.

I was still ambling along the main road when a police patrol car silently slid up beside me.

'You need any help, sir?' asked one of the policemen, hardly managing to suppress a smile.

'No thanks, just making my way home.' Apparently they had received a call from a lady who said that there was a poor soul wandering the streets in need of help.

'Where do you live, sir?'

'Near Seskinore Forest.'

'That figures,' whispered his mate, clearly about to crack up. 'Have you a carer?'

'Alan Titchmarsh,' I said, and they finally gave in to outright laughter, to the point where tears ran down the cheeks of the nearest.

'Why don't you just tell us what you are doing?' he asked in a marginally more controlled way. I explained the events to date and they seemed reassured.

'Would you like a lift back?'

'No, thanks, not far to go now.' The last thing I wanted was to be seen getting out of a patrol car in full camouflage gear. It would have been the talk of the village for months.

'Okay,' he said as they pulled away, 'be careful of ash dieback!'

Everyone's a joker, I thought.

'Can you smell slurry?' asked his mate.

At home, I finally removed the suit, doused it in petrol and, standing in wellingtons, vest and boxer shorts, I had the immense satisfaction of seeing the whole thing turn into a burning bush.

8

Fresh Pastures

By 2010, it was an absolute joy to walk amongst the woods, lakes and meadows observing the new residents. It is said that over time the average garden will be visited by 40 birds and 6 mammals. We were delighted to realise that our score by this time was 64 bird species and 12 mammals – very encouraging! The lakes had become the focal point of the project, attracting all manner of wildlife, including many aquatic insects.

We were quite happy to sit back and watch the garden mature when nature took an unexpected turn. The winter of 2010 was one of the harshest in recent years – snowfall came in late autumn to most of Northern Ireland and all manner of seasonal weather records were broken. 'Coldest November night ever recorded,' announced the early morning radio ... 'Traffic chaos as heavy snowfall closes the Glenshane Pass,' warned the newspaper headlines ... 'Don't travel unless you have to,' advised the police spokesman.

We looked out that first morning on to a changed landscape. It was magical and silent. There had been very heavy snow during the night and it had blanketed the woodlands, meadows and gardens. Familiar landmarks had disappeared; ugly sheds across the valley had been airbrushed out and mystical, crystal-covered scenery was crying out to be explored and enjoyed. The great pleasure on any snowy morning is to be the first to walk across the undisturbed surface and leave a trail of boot prints on what was, a second before, pristine and unblemished white. I am not sure why it is so satisfying, but we were soon in our boots and waterproofs, striding through the deep snow. Though we were thoroughly enjoying the outing, the real purpose of it was to see if there were any prints in the fresh snow that might indicate visiting wildlife that we were unaware of. We saw the trails of several pheasants, rooks and small birds, but the telltale pad marks of a fox were the most surprising. The single tracks, all in a straight line, were clear evidence that Reynard had been about, but it was the enormous distance he had covered during a single night that was most impressive. He had visited every hedgerow, path and meadow during his nocturnal rambling – it was clear proof of this fox's tenacity and resilience and shows why, in spite of years of persecution, large numbers of these predators still survive.

The snow and ice lasted for weeks. When the thaw came we realised that a combination of very low temperatures and wet ground had killed off many of the shrubs and trees we had planted. We lost many plants that, in normal circumstances, are considered fully frost hardy, and it was not pleasant work to pull up and burn the various casualties. All of the buddleias were gone, the parallel hedges of escallonia wiped out, many of the ornamental shrubs and some of the smaller conifers were dead – and all would have to be replaced. It was a frustrating setback because many of them were well established and already helping to create a more attractive habitat. We tried to meet these challenges with (in therapy parlance) 'radical acceptance': to accept that stuff happens, and that we just needed to get on with it!

Early on in 2010, some land adjoining our property was advertised for sale – nine acres of poorly drained, neglected land, which included a three-acre birch and ash wood. The price was reasonable and its inaccessible position made it unattractive to local farmers so we were the most interested purchasers. The land especially appealed because we knew it was once owned by Rosemary's father. However, we had tried to design the garden so that it would need only minimum maintenance – we'd planted shrubberies and woodland so that they'd need little attention, and only the cutting of grass in the summer months would be time consuming. If we purchased more land, what would we do with it, and could we manage it? We consulted our three sons and their advice was unanimous. Matt, in particular, advised us to protect our boundaries – we had already put too much into our project to risk someone coming alongside and setting up an enterprise that would undo our work.

In the event it took nearly two years to finalise the ownership of the land and the delays were frustrating to say the least. It is not unusual in Ireland for land to be exchanged between neighbours without the parties going to the expense of solicitors or drawing up new deeds. This can mean that the locally acknowledged ownership does not match the official paperwork. In the case of our new land, maps and revised deeds had to be drawn up, which all took time. The precise boundaries, rights of way and acreages of the land were unclear and needed to be recalculated – this is typical when land has been reclaimed from the bog years before but never formally registered. Papers and draft maps went between us, the Land Registry and other solicitors, and we imagined the final bill for all these transactions creeping up and up. However we saw the additional acreage would have huge potential as part of our overall project so we had no alternative but to stick with it.

We finally received the completed papers and set about trying to decide how these two additional fields and the three-acre wood would fit into our original scheme. We had of course discussed ideas for the new land, but didn't make any moves until ownership was confirmed. In the end, the decision was straightforward: to apply for a forestry grant to plant up both fields with trees so that they would eventually join up with the existing birch and ash forest to make a substantial woodland area. We had already planted well over a thousand trees – we believe that they are the most dynamic resource we have to address the damage being done to the natural environment. They have inherent strength in themselves – they absorb pollutants from the atmosphere, generate oxygen, stabilise soil and would eventually dry up our new land by preventing surface flooding. They are undoubtedly the way to breathe life back into damaged landscapes and enable wildlife to 'flow' through the countryside thus making vital habitat connections.

Purists sometimes like to make a distinction between native trees (that have evolved alongside our native wildlife and have developed ecological relationships), non-native (those brought here by humans) and naturalised (introduced trees which have been growing here for hundreds of years, e.g. the horse chestnut). We worried not about these distinctions because we were very happy to get any kind of trees to add to the habitat. With the support of the Woodland Trust we applied for the grant and it was agreed that the area was indeed suitable for planting with a selection of 'native' Irish trees.

Under the auspices of the Woodland Trust and the Department of Agriculture and Rural Development (DARD), we employed the local tree expert to design the scheme and oversee the work schedules. He was handsome and clean-cut, very neatly turned out, so I couldn't understand why everyone called him Woolly. At this stage I hadn't seen his name written down, so I presumed it was some kind of nickname, but it didn't seem to fit. In the end I spoke to one of his men. 'Why do you call the boss Woolly?'

'Because that's his name,' he said, looking slightly puzzled.

'But there's nothing woolly about him. How do you spell his name?'

'W-I-L-L-Y.'

I finally understood!

Getting used to the Northern Ireland accent had been tricky from the beginning, and I am sure local people had similar difficulty understanding everything I said. The breakthrough came when one local wag said, 'It's easy, Bob, at least in Belfast – all you have to remember is the phrase "I box with my hand". Substitute "o" for the "a" till it becomes "I bax with my hond" and you have it. Mind you, that solution won't work in Tyrone or Fermanagh!'

Willie – or Woolly – advised us that first of all we needed to put drains into both fields. We'd heard this before.

'Do you mean piped drains?' I asked, remembering the extensive work and the cost involved during our earlier efforts on the original site.

Thankfully not. Willy planned to design a network of trenches across the whole plot, depending on the natural slope of the land and the likely drainage patterns that already existed, and use a digger to do the excavation. He explained that the soil removed would be used to make raised piles every four feet or so and that he and his men would plant a tree on top of each mound. This would keep the new roots clear of any standing water and hopefully get the trees off to a flying start, with the plan that as they grew and their root systems developed, they would take up plenty of water and make this wet land markedly drier.

'What kind of trees do you suggest?' I asked.

'All native trees. I will use birch on that lower land which is very wet, alder and ash for the main hillside, and blocks of oak, rowan, hazel, red oak and pine to give variety and colour. The oaks particularly will help to support your wildlife project. What do you intend to do with that peaty land in the bottom of the valley?'

'Probably build another lake to join with the others.'

'Well, alders, birch and willows will thrive down there if you need some shelter around the water's edge.'

Our application was processed by DARD and Willie's team began work in the spring of 2012. A digger excavated a complex pattern of drains across both fields. We had asked that an avenue be left clear down the centre of each field, both for access and as a way of seeing any wildlife that might arrive. The clear areas would form a crossroads in the centre of the future wood and would provide a vantage point that covered four directions. We also asked for a space for access around the edges of each new planting.

A sizeable heap of assorted bundles of whips arrived; I asked Willie how long he thought the planting would take.

'We will be putting in approximately 4,500 trees so we should be finished by tomorrow lunchtime at the latest.'

'With only four men? Planting that many trees in so short a time?' I asked, remembering just how long it had taken us to set our whips in the early days.

'Watch them!' said Willie.

Each man took several bundles of whips and placed them in a carrying bag slung over their shoulders. They also held short handled spades. At walking pace and with very little hesitation, they opened up the top of each mound with the spade, pushed in a tree and closed up the soil with pressure from their boot. They were incredibly speedy and, as Willie had predicted, the two fields were fully planted in no time.

Since the field had been neglected for many years, there was extensive reed growth around these tiny trees that looked like it might be harmful.

'Will those reeds choke the new trees?' I asked Willie. 'Do they need removing?'

'They'll do no harm – in fact they help the young trees by providing shelter. A prolonged dry spell immediately after planting can sometimes be a problem and will kill off new trees, but if this happens we will replace any casualties next spring. Mass planting of this kind is the one instance where gardeners or farmers should wish for a wet summer!'

In fact, that summer turned out to be very wet and, out of four and a half thousand trees, we had only one casualty!

The established woodland that we had purchased as part of the deal consisted of mature silver birch, ash and willow. It was woodland that had developed on the edge of raised bogland and had matured naturally as centuries of leaf mould covered the peat. The remnants of an old raised laneway – probably constructed for access to the bog during peat digging – was still discernible along one edge of the wood, though most of its length was now impassable as it was covered with a dense tangle of brambles and thorn. The woodland was also divided at its centre by a wide, deep channel that had been excavated sometime in the past, presumably to help the drainage of the surrounding land. Plenty of the trees were not in perfect condition either – many of them had been completely blown over and had their roots exposed, or were broken halfway up their trunks, probably during winter storms over the years. Trees and parts of trees had fallen in a random fashion, sometimes one on top of the other, and a jungle of brambles had threaded through the branches in a way that made the wood virtually impossible to negotiate. The whole area had clearly been left to its own devices for many years and we realised that we would need to undertake some serious clearance of the forest floor before the natural regeneration found in healthy woodlands could take place. Dense ivy covered many of the trees and, as beginners in the business of creating sustainable habitats, this caused us a dilemma straight away. Should we remove the ivy or leave it? Once again we had to try to think things through.

It is common knowledge that ivy can damage bark as it climbs and will eventually completely take over even a mature tree. Its weight often weakens branches, and its growth prevents light getting through to the leaves of the host tree. During the winter it can act as a sail meaning that high winds can topple the entire tree or cause branches to snap. Many experts recommend keeping the ivy on the forest floor and at least three or four feet from the trunk; others argue that it's vital for wildlife. It gives good cover to nesting birds, and the berries that appear in November provide a food source for blackbirds, thrushes, redwings, collared doves and wood pigeon until April, a time when there is often little else on offer. Butterflies and small mammals also use ivy for shelter. In the end we decided to aim for a compromise – when we got around to tidying up this woodland we'd leave some ivy on the weak or diseased trees and remove it from the healthy specimens.

Although we believed that this area had been free of any human activity for many years, there was much less birdlife than we expected. We did spot wrens and tree creepers, and a pair of buzzards rearing their young in an enormous raft of a nest. In the winter months, woodcock came to the damp corners in numbers. But apart from these welcome species the place seemed relatively empty of birds.

In fact, the undergrowth was so dense that we probably missed many of the resident birds, but there were plenty of other things to excite our interest. Fallen trees and rotten wood were everywhere, and fungi of all kinds were active in breaking down the dead matter. Perfect specimens of bracket fungi adorned many trees and there was clear evidence, in the form of half-eaten edges on odd ones, that they were part of the diet of some woodland dweller. In addition, there were many fairy-tale red-capped fly agaric toadstools, shaggy inkcaps in abundance and boletes of various types. Speckled wood butterflies, bees, moths, beetles, spiders and bugs we could not identify were everywhere and at dusk bats flittered about. Bright green mosses and lichen clung to most trees and these mini-jungles were home to all manner of insects.

One particular dell was really inaccessible and had probably not been visited by anyone for many years. The trunks and root systems of the birch and willow jumbled together and were totally covered in rich, green moss. It was a silent, enchanting place; a wildwood where the solitude was palpable and the imagination knew no bounds. Sitting within this emerald enclosure it was easy to be transported back to times when wolves, enormous deer and bears roamed the land, and pollution and pesticides were not on anyone's radar.

Before any work could begin on the trees it was necessary to tackle the brambles. They were too established, too dense, for strimmers so we realised we would have to take radical action and use a specific bramble spray. This would cause the brambles to die back, and then we'd be able to clear them. We hated chemical control of any kind, but believed we had no other option if we wanted light to get to the forest floor to help regeneration in the long term. We planned to cut the fallen timber into logs and pile the smaller, brittle branches (or brash) into heaps as cover or nesting sites. We'd leave the rotting trees with the bracket fungus as they seemed to be doing no harm and would fall down at some point anyway.

Two of our sons, Matt and Howard, have London-based careers, but love the opportunity to get over to Ireland. They exchanged pinstripes for boiler suits and got busy tidying up the newly acquired woodland. We soon had the area cleared. They both felt there was something hugely rewarding about working amongst mature trees, especially in a forest such as this, that has been untouched by humans for decades. The comfortable smell of damp leaves, the dappled light, the silence and the feeling that the hard work is making an impact is tremendously satisfying. Sitting down for a break in the open air with a cup of tea, Cheddar cheese and home-made fruit cake is also something else.

The first task was to get access to the old raised lane way so we used saws and the strimmer to clear a pathway along its length. As we progressed it was evident that in the past this entrance into the bogland had been used as a dumping ground for old cars. We found four or five rusting carcasses entangled with briars. This discovery was in no way out of the ordinary because across much of Ireland, once the digging of peat had ceased, boglands were often seen as useless tracts of land. The accessible parts became places to dump all manner of rubbish, especially old vehicles or builders' debris. There was no way for us to remove these rusting hulks because they were just too entwined with vegetation so we decided instead to try to camouflage them with the branches and brash we were clearing. Perhaps one day we will be able to get rid of them completely; for now they stand as a reminder that anything discarded in the countryside stays as litter for years. We also found barbed wire everywhere – hammered into trees, tangled into the grassy banks and strung between rotting posts. There were also flags of black plastic caught on trees, old fertiliser bags and an assortment of farm rubbish that looked totally out of place in wild woodland of this type. One winter the tree holding the buzzard's nest collapsed and even their huge platform of a nest was laced through with blue and orange nylon string.

Once one section of the woodland was cleared of the bramble cover, we discovered the remains of an old badger sett with linked tunnels and holes, but it had clearly been unoccupied for many years. So far we have only seen one badger but there is a thriving colony a mile away in Seskinore Forest so with luck they may rediscover our wood and return some day. The same goes for sika deer. We spotted one crossing the meadow, and found prints, but so far no regular visitors have been attracted to our garden. We wait in expectation!

The unpredictability of the outcome is a surprisingly appealing aspect of trying to attract wildlife. On odd days, even after all of our earlier efforts, the land could still seem fairly devoid of activity. Nothing would be moving and we often wondered where all our regulars had gone. As the garden became more established, these quiet spells became shorter and shorter – within hours there would always be a bird to spot or a butterfly to try to identify. We celebrated every new arrival, and the more unexpected the newcomer, the more we rejoiced.

As an example, Ian – a neighbour and skilled tree man – was helping to trim some of the tangled lower branches in the mature birch wood when he almost stepped on a woodcock. The bird exploded into flight and jinked and swerved as it flew directly towards where I stood motionless. It must have mistaken my dull green coat and brown hat for a natural part of the forest because it pitched in and landed not three feet away. Its plumage, almost identical to the colours and shapes on the forest floor made it instantly invisible, except for its unblinking large brown eye. Three more came out of the undergrowth near where Ian was working and the one at my feet eventually jumped up and headed after them.

'Four of them all within a few yards,' said Ian, 'but that's woodcock for you. Birds everywhere one minute, not a feather to be seen the next!'

It is true that, along with the nightjar, the woodcock ranks as one of the most mysterious and magical birds. I explained to Ian that during the spring at our house in Sherwood Forest the male birds would follow a circular flight path over the garden and trees. This mating display flight, known as 'roding', was so regular and reliable that it was possible, at dusk, to set a watch by the arrival of the first flighting bird. The twisick note, issued at very regular intervals by each bird, carried a good distance on a still night. For us, as lovers of wild things, the sight of this bird with its bat-like flight completing the circuits was a real thrill. Country lore also holds that woodcock chicks ride on the back of flying birds – and more than one old countryman claims to have witnessed this. It is also believed by these old timers that woodcock will never step over fallen branches or obstacles on the woodland floor. At the turn of the century, hunters used this knowledge to guide the birds into traps or 'springes'. They would build a giant V-shape of branches on the forest floor and place the trap at the narrow exit point.

Woodcock migrate from Norway and other northern countries

as winter arrives and can appear in large numbers in Ireland during an east wind or when temperatures fall in Scandinavia. Although their numbers have diminished in recent years, the cause for this decline isn't clear, so the woodcock is a species that we need to watch carefully. Unlike pheasants or wildfowl, these birds cannot be hand-reared in large numbers: their young leave the nests as soon as they hatch and need access to small worms and soft ground immediately in order to survive. The fall in the numbers of woodcock is worrying because far too many species, such as the grey partridge, have already disappeared from much of the UK and Ireland with hardly a whimper from anyone.

This fate is also true of the red grouse. We have heard that there were red grouse on the bogland to the side of us, and it is well documented that there were thriving populations on the Fivemiletown Mountain a few miles away thirty years ago. They have all gone now and I doubt they will ever come back!

The rapid decline in grouse populations might be due to causes beyond modern agriculture. Populations began to tumble during the early years of the last century and the birds totally disappeared from many moors where they had once been numerous. Hunting them had become suddenly popular, especially for the wealthy, and the spread of railways to the more remote regions where the grouse thrived made access much easier. The development of driven shooting on these moorlands inevitably followed – huge teams of beaters were recruited, squads of keepers hired and favoured mountains rented at considerable cost. By the 1920s, it had become the height of fashion to be seen in these regions during August and September and at peak times special trains from the major cities were laid on to accommodate the sudden increase in passengers and dogs heading for the north and west. It has been estimated that at the peak of grouse shooting's popularity, the first few weeks of each new season would claim over one and a half million brace of birds – a massive total, difficult to comprehend or condone today.

Grouse have always been prone to acute population changes and in August each year predictions would be made in the major newspapers about the numbers of birds observed and the prospects for the coming season. It was believed that these seasonal swings were due in part to the weather, but mainly to the actions of predators. A philosophy emerged that aimed to eliminate everything that might potentially have an impact on grouse numbers. Foxes, wildcats, badgers, polecats and otters were hunted relentlessly and many raptors, such as eagles, peregrines, harriers and buzzards, were virtually wiped out on the grouse moors. The planting of large blocks of coniferous forest on open moorland also reduced the natural habitat of the grouse.

However, science has shown us that the real culprit was a tiny white parasitic worm, not shooting, or loss of heather or forestry. The grouse pick these up as eggs from the shoots of heather and they multiply rapidly inside the birds. When grouse are plentiful so are the worms – as a consequence, a good year is often followed by a rapid decline in populations. As with woodcock, there is no simple way of hand-rearing grouse and it is difficult to see that these spectacular birds will ever return to our part of the world.

Once the old, neglected woodland was cleared as much as possible, our attention turned to the wet land at the foot of the valley. The stream, which issued from the bordering bogland and fed the two existing lakes, ran through this marshy ground and it seemed the perfect place to excavate a further lake. Lawrence and another driver arrived with two diggers, one the standard model, the other a specialist machine with extra wide tracks for working wet, peaty land. The idea was that the material scooped out would be placed on the hillside, with the feeder stream widened in order to ensure a continuous supply of fresh water throughout the year. We hoped that once the new lake had filled there would be a constant overflow which would move through the existing lake system before returning eventually to its original course further down the valley. We intended to go down to ten feet at one end and then gradually reduce the depth to two feet at the shallow end. Two islands would be left for nesting birds and tree planting.

The excavation went smoothly and, in less than three days, the project was completed and the new lake began to fill. Sitting at the foot of the valley and bordered on the lower side by a birch spinney and on the hillside by the newly planted mixtures of native trees, this addition to the landscape is in full sun for most of the day. It should eventually be a wonderfully sheltered place to sit and enjoy some solitude – which is what gardens and watching wildlife should be about.

However all gardens have to evolve over time. Our garden began purely as an attempt to create a sanctuary for wildlife but when our first grandchildren came along it also had to become an outside classroom, a place where the kids could experience nature at first-hand. Accompanying Joe and Izzy and, more recently, Arthur, around the woodlands, meadows and garden can often take up to four hours as they climb trees, and learn about fungi, birds, wild flowers or whatever it is that catches their attention. The more they understand, the more their interest and innate curiosity grows. The old woodland, especially, is the place where their imaginations know no bounds, and mystery and myth combine effortlessly with reality. Most children have an innate love of nature and the outdoors but this curiosity has to be nurtured and encouraged. It seems a pity that many young people seem to have become distanced from the natural world around them and are gadget-dependent and housebound much of the time. Understandably, many parents are fearful of giving children the freedom to roam that earlier generations had, but the development of teaching outdoors in modern primary schools has shown that given opportunity, children do respond enthusiastically. Learning outdoors, whether facilitated by parents or teachers, does excite the curiosity of children and stimulates all their senses in a way that indoor learning cannot. It is also first-rate exercise!

In a similar way, as the garden has matured, the woodlands and meadows have become a haven for the adults in our family – a place to escape and to take time away from the busy schedules that come with earning a living. Howard and his wife, Cathy, have especially busy commitments in London, and coming back to the sanctuary of the countryside always seems to recharge their batteries. Perhaps we could all benefit from 'turning the clock back' a little and enjoying places where solitude, contemplation and relaxation are the order of the day?

With the family in mind, we built a changing hut on the lakeside, purchased canoes and a small boat with an electric engine, and constructed a pontoon and diving board for wild swimming during the summer. A friend provided three surplus picnic benches. The area has become a wonderful place to have some fun on a hot day. Using the garden in this way appears to have little impact on the wildlife, especially the butterflies, damselflies and dragonflies – which the new lake attracted to our garden in numbers for the first time – and half an hour after our aquatic activity ends, the moorhens and duck are back and the trout begin to rise.

As well as the dragonflies and damselflies, the building of the latest lake brought other new arrivals. One afternoon when I was watching a heron stalk the margins it suddenly made a lightning strike and came up with an eel that wound itself around the bird's long beak as it endeavoured to escape. The heron eventually subdued it by hammering it against the trunk of a nearby willow and then swallowed it whole. Even more surprisingly, a few weeks after this, I found a dead river lamprey in the reed beds.

One warm July afternoon when we were showing some friends around the garden, the first kingfisher appeared, a darting bolt of turquoise, piping a warning whistle before skimming along just above the surface of the water. Local ornithologists had no record of them in our area.

Feeding the margins of the lakes also paid dividends as mallard and teal would flight in at dusk each evening to seek out the grains. There is something very special about sitting near water as the light fades, waiting to see if any wildfowl arrive. The birdsong ceases, usually the blackbirds are the last to roost and there is a lull as the world falls silent. Where the duck stay during the day is a mystery but, as the light fades, they return. The dogs will always hear them first, both heads turning in unison to look up at the darkening sky. They fidget in expectation as a party of five duck arrive in a rush of wings, as if from nowhere. One second nothing, the next the mallard are skimming across the last of the lighted sky in search of a landing place. Sometimes the display can be spellbinding, especially on cold, still nights when the sound of their arrival is like the whoosh of an express train. The teal always arrive late, flitting about like bats until they drop in to feed. As we sit and wait to enjoy this nightly ritual, we never forget that just a few years ago the land held nothing and it is comforting to know that it is largely our efforts that have changed things. Given a fighting chance, wildlife is astonishingly resilient and watching these wild duck arrive at dusk, or years ago seeing woodcock flying their display routes, reminds us that some of the simplest pleasures can also be the most rewarding.

Speaking of bats, they have been active around the house and over the lakes right from the beginning and we see them every evening during the summer months. One weekend in early September, the local biodiversity officer asked me to lead a guided 'Bat Walk' through Seskinore Forest. A sizeable party of wildlife enthusiasts gathered and we walked through the trees until dark. Though the forest is home to plenty of bats, unusually, on this occasion, we did not see a single one. I worked hard trying to keep the group motivated by saying things like 'there are usually some down by the lake' or 'they will come out at dusk' but during the whole ramble none appeared. The next day when I opened up a black parasol sunshade on the courtyard at the rear of the house, five pipistrelle bats emerged. That's wildlife for you – unpredictable but totally fascinating!

With the acquisition of the new land our site had grown to seventeen acres and describing where wildlife had been seen or work needed doing became a bit confusing, until an unplanned, ad hoc naming system emerged. The trend started with bridges. The channel that fed the lakes from the bogland was too wide to jump comfortably so Rosemary's cousin Brian built a bridge with handrails that instantly became known as Brian's Bridge. Crossing the wide channel inside the mature wood needed a substantial metal structure, designed and welded together by Rosemary's brother – Kevin's Bridge. The crossing that spanned the overflow between the lakes became Joe's Bridge and the small footbridge near the bogland is Izzy's. We need a further bridge to cross a deep ditch near the new plantings and I am sure that in time this will be named after our third grandchild, Arthur. We now also have the Daffodil Walk, the Pheasant Tunnel, the Old Bog Lane and the Wild Wood. No doubt there will be many more.

9
Moving On

A one-and-a-half acre field that was part of the original land we bought is an excellent example of one of the key themes of our project – progressing by trial and error. The first year we had it ploughed and seeded with game crop, a mixture of maize, sorghum, millet, kale and sunflowers that was recommended in several of the books on wildlife gardening we consulted. The seed was very expensive but we hoped that the outcome would be a supply of winter food and cover for pheasants. Though everything grew, the field was only visited by a few finches and their interest seemed to last for just a matter of days. We have since learnt that there are in fact different game crop mixtures to suit latitude, microclimate and position so we probably chose the wrong one but at the time it was all that was available. We thought we might give game crop another try some time in the future.

The next thing we tried were sunflowers. Wood pigeon came to the field for a day or so after the seed was set, no doubt to seek out anything left on the surface, but the wet, cool summer that year meant there was a very poor germination and the bright yellow flower heads were few and far between. Growing sunflowers successfully in our part of Northern Ireland requires a warm dry spring and a good summer – conditions that only come around every few years – so that first attempt was another spectacular failure. We did much better with sunflowers later on, but each year was a gamble with unpredictable weather determining the eventual outcome.

Our third attempt came via a kindly neighbour. He was

sowing barley on an adjacent field and, since he had grain to spare, suggested a solution. 'I've got the machinery here and some extra seed. Would you like me to sow it in your small field to help your wildlife project? No cost!'

We were of course very pleased with his generous offer and in no time the field was ploughed, harrowed and planted with barley. This crop grew perfectly and, by September, was rich with grain, which we left on the plants for winter feeding for the birds. The first storms of the winter flattened the standing crop and the rooks arrived in their thousands. This is rook country with an enormous colony, once the largest in the UK, only a few miles away and soon the barley field was black with the feeding birds and there were hundreds more swirling around in the air above. For three days the field became a set on a Hitchcock film, but once the feast was over, the birds left just as quickly as they had arrived, without having missed a single grain of barley. This bonanza certainly helped the rooks, but as a winter food source for other species it was yet another failure!

We didn't mind this because we regard rooks as fascinating birds. They are often seen as villains, especially in urban gardens where they can clear a bird table in seconds, but the more we watched them the more fascinating we found them. From a distance they look matt black, but when the sun shines their plumage looks varnished, with underlying tones of purple, mauve, blue and bronze. They are intelligent, ingenious and sociable – and their antics on our bird tables led us to respect their persistence and cunning. Some of our bird feeders hang from the edge of the bird table and the rooks learned to swing them like a pendulum until they gained enough momentum to shake the peanuts free or dislodge the whole feeder from the hook. We fixed the feeders on with string and the rooks unpicked the knots. In the end we decided their resourcefulness deserved reward and simply put wheat on the table for them.

When the wind is strong and coming from a certain direction

they appear in their hundreds and clearly take great pleasure in using the currents for their amazing aerobatics. They wheel, pirouette and soar in obvious delight, and these displays can go on for many minutes. Most spectacular of all is the day the young birds leave the nearby rookery – we always stand and watch in wonder as young and old tumble about the sky. It's a combination of tuition, social support and pure joy.

Of course, as the raids on our barley field demonstrated, they can be a pest on grain fields, especially after bad weather when the corn has been blown over or 'laid'. Indeed in the past, they were often known as 'corn crows' and, if we were being pedantic, scarecrows should properly be called 'scarerooks'. They are normally omnivores, feeding on grassland invertebrates and more recently on picnic sites and rubbish dumps but, in my opinion at least, their reputation as pests is not entirely deserved.

Traditionally, young birds were taken from the rookeries just before they flew to be made into rook pie; the dish was said by many to be deliciously gamey and a little like rabbit. Years ago I was invited to a rook and nettle pie supper and was pleasantly surprised at the taste. I said to the man sitting next to me, 'This is really good!'

'That's because it is steak and spinach,' he replied with a grin. 'Nothing wild in it!'

One wildlife sideshow to the rook invasion on our barley crop came when I was standing at the edge of the field trying to get a few good pictures of the massed flocks. A female sparrowhawk cleared the hedge and knocked over a full-grown rook. The bird looked markedly bigger than the hawk, but the power of the impact seemed to totally stun the victim and the sparrowhawk then lifted it into the hedge bottom to complete the kill. The whole thing was over in seconds, and was a classic demonstration of the power, agility and efficiency of these impressive aerial predators.

We then had the bright idea of just leaving the field to its own devices but it is extraordinary in this part of the world just how quickly untended pasture turns into reed-filled meadowland that few wildlife species seem to find attractive. This part of our plan is still a work in progress – we will keep experimenting to find the crop that provides the best cover and the most sustainable food source. Perhaps, in the end, the planting of more trees on this small field might prove to be the answer.

One gardening chore we had not foreseen when designing the garden was keeping the orchard fruit trees free of long grass. Normally it is recommended that at least one square metre of soil around each tree is kept clear of grass and weeds, which in our case meant strimming three or four times a year – adding another chore to the maintenance workload. We decided a few hens to keep down the vegetation would be the answer, so we purchased a henhouse and some birds on the point of lay. Two were lost to foxes almost immediately so we were forced to enclose the whole orchard with wire netting and protect the base with an electric fence. The finished construction looked a little like Stalag Luft III but it worked and, though fox prints were regularly seen around the perimeter, the poultry remained safe. In fact we both knew very little about poultry keeping but the care of the hybrid Sussex and Braekel hens became part of our daily routine in the garden, and they did a good job of keeping the orchard tidy. Watching them soon became strangely addictive.

We had been warned by the local poultry expert, who said, 'Once you start keeping hens you will always want some around the place. They are fascinating to watch and very relaxing. Some folks hate being woken up by the dawn crowing of the cockerel but I feel it seems to fit perfectly with living in the countryside and I wouldn't be without a rooster. In any case, real eggs are truly something else!'

Our poultry enterprise came to an abrupt end a couple of years later. The remaining two hens were ageing and had virtually stopped laying. We were undecided what to do about this when fate took a hand. Unbeknownst to us the battery on the electric fence ran out, a passing fox must have tested the wire, no doubt as it did most evenings, found the current gone, bitten through the cable, wriggled under the wire and taken the poultry. The episode was upsetting at the time but it solved our immediate dilemma and I am sure we will get back to keeping hens again sometime in the near future.

In the spring of 2015 we were taking our morning tea and toast in our usual spot when the first Irish hares turned up. A pair crossed the lawn and sat looking down towards the lakes. Hares had not been seen in this part of the country for years and their arrival was both unexpected and truly exciting. Seeing these animals may not seem too exceptional to those living in the parts of Ireland or the UK where these are still plentiful but here they are rare and we celebrated their appearance on our plot. They seemed to emerge from the wild flower meadow and, since Irish hares generally have a fairly limited range, we hoped they would stay around and take advantage of the sympathetic habitat we had provided. A dream at that time was that one day they would breed on our land.

They don't use burrows, but will make 'forms' or shallow depressions, often in dense vegetation such as rushes, heather or tall grass, in sheltered locations. This means that often the hare is only seen when it is 'flushed' from its form moments before it is likely to be trodden on. Females can produce two to three litters a year with numbers born ranging from one to four. Gestation period is about fifty days. Unlike rabbits, leverets (baby hares) are born above ground. They are fully furred and their eyes are open, and to begin with they hide in thick vegetation. In order to protect them from being detected by predators their mother will only feed them once a day, usually around dusk. The litter stays together for the first few days, but then will disperse to the surrounding area. Leverets grow rapidly but infant mortality is high, so when we see young hares we keep our fingers firmly crossed.

How times change! My early years were spent in England where, in the richest farming country with its crops of wheat, sugar beet and barley, hares were numerous and were generally regarded as an agricultural pest. These were brown hares, cousins of the Irish hare. In the 1970s and 80s, landowners organised seasonal 'hare drives' to control numbers. At the end of the game shooting season it was traditional for shooting men, farmers and beaters to get together in teams of thirty or so to work the open arable fields with a walk-and-wait system. One team would flush the hares from the ploughed land while the waiting guns would be positioned five or six fields away to ambush the fleeing animals. The shooting was seldom challenging because the hares were moving slowly, no doubt believing that they had escaped any danger. Indeed many were shot as they stopped running and sat. I never took part in these forays because they were certainly not to my taste – they killed far too many animals (one estate shot 348, 276 and 197 hares on three successive days), which I felt threatened the survival of the species in the region and certainly did not sit well with the idea of any partnership between sport and conservation.

Thankfully these outings are a thing of the past and many organisations have been formed to preserve both Irish and brown hares because populations are thought to have suffered a serious decline during the past ten to twenty years. How many times have we heard the comment that there used to be plenty of hares around but that they haven't been seen in years?

The reduction in numbers has been attributed to factors such as loss of rushes or hedgerows that provide cover; conversion of pasture that contained many different grasses to that which has only ryegrass; greater disturbance through high stocking levels of cattle; and deaths from faster farm machinery. In addition, increased predation from foxes and crows plus the increased traffic on roads have all played a part in the disappearance of hares across the UK and Ireland. Hares are fascinating and engaging animals that are thought to have arrived when the Ice Age retreated and to have been around for ten thousand years. We truly hope they go on to prosper in this part of Tyrone. Their presence was certainly welcome on our little patch and in the following years it was wonderful to see them breed successfully and become permanent residents on our land!

It was also about this time that we saw rabbits again. We had noticed odd ones in the early days but they always died out through liver disease; these latest arrivals seemed to have developed some immunity, and they thrived. Scrapes, where the animals dig out small holes to get at the edible tree roots, began to appear everywhere and seeing their white scuts bobbing away into the undergrowth became a daily occurrence during our morning walks.

Normally rabbits dig a warren of burrows but on our land there was no evidence of this. Those which had moved in seemed content to stay above ground in the thick cover. They multiplied rapidly and we got used to seeing impressive numbers of them on the lawns and shrubberies, usually at dawn or dusk. We took real pleasure in their antics as new actors in the wildlife soap opera – until they discovered our vegetable patch!

Growing vegetables has been a mixture of highs and lows. The 'grow your own' movement, with its persuasive advertising, makes it all sound so attractive and straightforward, but this has not been our experience. To begin with, the soil in our vegetable plot was heavy clay mixed with some subsoil and the drainage was very poor. After any prolonged rainfall it was soon sodden and useless for successful crop production. Over the years we have added grit and masses of organic material and, though it is now in much better shape, it is still far from ideal. We are largely self-providing during the summer months but there have been many hard lessons to learn along the way.

We decided that March 2005, ten months after moving into the house, was a good time to make a determined effort with vegetable growing. We sowed a rectangular patch with Bunyard's Exhibition broad beans and we waited in excited expectation for the first dark rubbery leaves to push up through the surface. Nothing appeared. We waited another week. Still nothing! The answer to this gardening puzzle was simple. When we scratched beneath the surface we found the remains of our broad bean seeds. Now we needed to work out who were the culprits. We set up a humane cage trap complete with a few beans one evening and next morning two wood mice were inside. Now we know what these little animals can do, we have to start peas, broad beans, runner beans, French beans and courgettes in the greenhouse and plant them out as growing plants to avoid them being consumed by Mickey and his mates!

In addition to the beans, our annual selection of vegetables for the plot is very traditional: Charlotte and King Edward potatoes, turnips, swedes, Jerusalem artichokes and beetroot. We buy lettuce, cabbage, Brussels sprouts and kale as plants from the local market. It is a system that has worked well, and knowing the produce is totally organic is comforting. Furthermore, walking around the supermarket vegetable shelves and saying, 'We don't need that, we have our own,' gave a very smug feeling. That is until the return of the rabbits!

When we first constructed the raised beds for vegetables, we built a rabbit-proof fence around the whole vegetable patch, although at that stage there weren't any rabbits about. The plot was very near to open country and the fence was a precaution against potential attacks, but stepping over it became a practical nuisance. A year before the rabbits reappeared I spent a whole day digging it out ... That's the unpredictability of wildlife gardening for you – we spend twelve years complaining about the inconvenience of the rabbit fence, finally remove it and then the next year the rabbits appear in numbers!

During their nightly visits they decimated the cabbage plants, chopped off the broccoli heads, ate the curly kale plants and hammered the Brussels sprouts. We replanted and covered the new vegetables with wire netting, but the rabbits were persistent and the end result was the same. By the time the rabbits found the French beans and runner beans, they were growing well up the canes. The rabbits left the runner beans for reasons unknown, but destroyed the French ones by chewing the stems at the base. It was pretty soul-destroying to see the withered remains still clinging to the poles. Living with wildlife sometimes involves compromise so I will need to rebuild the fence in the near future!

Visiting gardeners often ask how we deal with slugs on our heavy ground. I wish we could give a simple answer. The slugs rarely bother our root crops, and we try to protect our brassicas by planting them out only when they're well advanced and by surrounding them with ashes from our wood-burning stove to dry up the surface of the soil. When these measures haven't worked well enough we've tried upturned grapefruit, spreading eggshells, sinking pots full of lager and picking them up at night with the aid of a torch but nothing is totally guaranteed. Slugs and magpies are the only thing we kill in the garden – we dispatch them with some reluctance because we believe that everything has its place in the wildlife chain – but in this damp climate, without some control on the patch, it would be almost impossible to grow vegetables. Perhaps the most wildlife-friendly – and enjoyable – approach would be to sit back and drink the beer while the hedgehogs and thrushes do their worst!

New visitors continued to arrive on our patch. We were excited to register successful hatchings of jays, blackcaps, whitethroats, warblers and spotted flycatchers. These last were always fascinating to watch – they nested close to the house and, when feeding their young, their energy and ability to chase and take the flying insects – including bees, wasps and butterflies – was always something special. Numbers of these long-range migrants from Africa have declined markedly in recent years; the cause is unclear, but hopefully various projects that are underway will find some answers and bring in strategies to protect these wonderful little birds.

It was pleasing to see the increase in the number of jays because the crow family has suffered from a degree of muddled thinking in the past few years. Jays, though now fully protected in Northern Ireland, have in the past attracted some hostility from sportsmen and gamekeepers because of their habit of nest-raiding during spring time. In fact, the bird is largely vegetarian and, though it was once frequently shot, it was always questionable just how much damage it did. In a similar fashion, the jackdaw is still regularly persecuted though there is little evidence that it does much widespread harm to game rearing or anything else. It's certainly a much less prolific egg stealer than some of its close cousins.

Although we were happy to see the jays and jackdaws, we felt much less happy about the numbers of grey crows and magpies on our land. Both species are amazingly adept at finding nests or newly hatched chicks and once they find a new nest will return daily until everything has been tracked down and devoured. In some areas these birds have become numerous and can be seen systematically quartering hedgerows and moorlands in order to seek out any nesting birds. Last year I saw a fifteen-strong brood of day-old pheasant chicks crossing our drive and watched as a pair of grey crows relentlessly targeted them. By the next afternoon the family had been halved and, I am sure, would have been wiped out totally if I hadn't chased off the crows. Magpie predation is also a serious threat but controversy surrounds this bird and there is some dispute whether it has any serious impact on songbird populations. Certainly the number of these birds has increased across Ireland in the last thirty years and when we first purchased the land they were here in significant numbers. In fact, on several occasions in the early days, we witnessed parties of them searching our hedgerows in springtime, leaving destroyed nests in their wake. We have absolutely no direct scientific evidence to support the theory that these black-and-white predators reduce the number of small birds but once we trapped and shot a number, the increase in the songbird population was clearly evident, although this might also have been thanks to the improved habitat.

We had deliberately planted the trees close together so that we would see results fairly quickly, understanding that some trees would need to be removed as everything matured. This occurred more quickly than we could have expected and we decided to create a ride down the centre of a wood that had become really dense. We hired a commercial chipper machine to clear a route through the planting and created a new pathway with the shredded material. We planted a thousand Tête-à-Tête daffodils alongside the new pathway and the enterprise gave us another lovely track to amble along each morning. Pheasants seemed to like this woodland glade habitat and since we regularly saw two or three scratching about in the area, we decided this would be a good spot to distribute grain during the winter months. The results were astonishing. Within weeks twenty or so birds were there every morning waiting like domestic hens for the arrival of their breakfast. We realised, of course, that the majority of these birds were likely to be semi-tame reared pheasants from the nearby shoot but hoped if they found sanctuary, a regular food source and adequate nesting sites, they would stay and go on to breed.

It was about this time that we spotted the first grey squirrel out in the open, although we had seen them on the trail camera. They were numerous in the nearby forest, but it had taken nearly ten years for the animals to venture into our plot. The introduced grey squirrel is not always the most popular because of the damage they do to young trees, their egg-stealing habits and their impact on the native red squirrel. It has long been thought that the greys drive out the more popular native red squirrels and that they carry the squirrel pox virus from which they are immune, but that is usually fatal to their red cousins. As a consequence they have been trapped and shot for many years. Many modern researchers argue that years of culling 'greys' has, in practice, had little impact on their overall numbers. They also argue that the decline of the native squirrel is caused more by deforestation, disease and severe winters than by competition from their American relatives. In our case we were happy to see this new arrival but will wait with interest to see if grey squirrels become regular visitors and if so, how they will interact with the other long-time residents.

One rather sad postscript to this new arrival came from an elderly neighbour, who told us, 'The block of forestry nearest to your property was felled five years before you came and that was alive with red squirrels. I don't know where they went when the trees came down.'

10
Winning Ways

It is a perfect October day: a cloudless blue sky, windless, with the air outside so clean and crisp it is pure joy to fill my lungs. The Irish countryside looks truly beautiful at this time of year as the autumnal colours of red oaks, maples, copper beech and larch contrast with the permanent deeper greens of the Austrian pines and noble firs. We are sitting on the upper storey of the tower at the front of the house and taking our early morning tea – loose tea, brewed lovingly in a proper pot – and wholemeal toast with home-made marmalade. When we are at home, this is a ritual we have followed almost every day since we started this project over fourteen years ago.

The view from this vantage point has become spectacular over the years and seeing it afresh each morning never disappoints. In the foreground, gravel paths lead to formal steps, with circular golden box hedges, rose arches and a birdbath, before heading down between the terraced slopes to the lake in the valley. The path is contained between parallel clipped Portuguese laurel and leads the eye gently towards the willows, bamboo and water beyond. On either side of the lawns the hedges have thickened into spinneys and the seven thousand or so trees we have planted create the illusion of unbroken woodland all the way to Seskinore Forest in the distance. Many of the trees are now over twenty feet high and though the rowans, holly and hawthorn have already been stripped of their berries, their mature silhouettes now give permanence to the landscape. The morning light, 'artist's light', creates intriguing patterns and shapes across the garden and, as we had hoped many years before, it is now impossible to determine where our property ends and the land beyond begins. Three thoroughbreds quietly grazing in the neighbour's field add to the picture. It is now a landscape to delight the senses. We never tire of renewing our acquaintance with it each new morning.

Its maturity contrasts sharply with the barren pastures that were here before, but the pleasure we take from seeing the garden develop pales into insignificance when we see what else is in it. This morning, for instance, as we sit with breakfast, we see five rabbits, three Irish hares, eleven pheasants (some perched on the rose arch), a dozen rooks, a jay, two magpies, four collared doves, a buzzard, and numerous small birds and wood pigeons. In the lake are over twenty mallard, truly wild birds that flight in at dusk every evening and leave en masse next morning to go who knows where. Some instinctive signal triggers their departure – they jump from the water together and disappear, usually while we are on our second piece of toast. Yesterday morning the moorhens were present, the day before two otters played in the lake – the daily variations are endless but always deeply satisfying. To date we have identified sixty-four species of birds living in the garden or visiting regularly (we don't count those just flying over), twelve mammals, and all manner of flying insects, butterflies and moths. Our hope to create a better, more sustainable wildlife habitat has already far exceeded our wildest dreams and we have certainly come a long way from the place where we started. However, one of the joys of creating a garden, especially when it involves wildlife, is that it is work in progress. It is a never-ending journey, highly satisfying to have come this far, but each day we still wait in anticipation to see what turns up next.

Though initially we set out in the hope of turning the clock back and trying to create a habitat that would attract and sustain wildlife, working towards achieving this goal has resulted in many peripheral outcomes we could not have predicted. The first of these concerns retirement.

During the first years of our marriage, we were typical of the great majority of people starting out. Setting up home, family, career and all of the other pressures create a tempo of life that is hectic and all-consuming. Most of us are forced on to a career treadmill, often aiming towards some kind of pinnacle. Whether we reach that pinnacle or not, it can be difficult to reach retirement and feel that we are yesterday's people, no longer on the fast track. This feeling, of course, can bring a great sense of loss, as one of our rural neighbours found. He had quite a prestigious job but in almost every conversation he would mention how much he was looking forward to retiring – something we hear often. In fact, he has spent his retirement so far watching daytime television – in some ways, it seems as though he has lost his identity.

Rosemary and I never saw retirement as an ending – in fact, retirement isn't really a word in our vocabulary. Instead, we saw the end of our main careers as an opportunity for a new beginning and a change of direction. We looked forward to a 'mixed portfolio' of family, charity work, sport, travel and learning new skills. For example, after a very successful career in education Rosemary completed a two-year course of study to become a cognitive behavioural therapist, and is now working in this field.

We couldn't have anticipated, though, that the creation of our wildlife garden would be a conduit to so many new activities and interests that, in some ways, are just as challenging and absorbing as our earlier careers.

That early search for help and information about other wildlife gardens, and the subject in general, meant we built up contacts with agencies we felt might be able to give us some guidance. These included local biodiversity officers, the RSPB, the Woodland Trust, organic garden societies and many others. In 2009 one of the biodiversity officers entered our developing habitat into the Northern Ireland RSPB environmental planning competition and, though we were runners-up, the publicity resulting from this accolade meant that for the first time the garden and what we were trying to achieve was in the public domain. Almost immediately secretaries of garden societies got in touch to ask if we would give talks on wildlife gardening and our project in particular. Interest in the subject was widespread, possibly because of the growing awareness of environmental destruction and the increasing alarm at the number of birds and insects now in serious decline. Conversations usually went something like this:

'We would like you to visit our society to talk about creating a better habitat for wildlife.'

'We are happy to come as long as you realise that, although we are passionate about wildlife, we are complete amateurs.'

'But we would like to hear about your practical experience. Your case study.'

It was always difficult to refuse and at the end of the talk would come the inevitable question: 'Would it be possible for us to visit your garden sometime in the future?'

With no planning whatsoever our post-retirement mixed portfolio had expanded into lecture tours, garden visits, radio broadcasts and now, in response to many requests, this book.

The gardeners and folks interested in conservation and wildlife are lovely without exception, and meeting them has been a great pleasure. Some remarks people have made stick in my mind: 'This garden upsets me because it is alive and has so much activity. Mine is meticulous and colourful, but it is sterile. I need to rethink things!'

Or, 'I see many aspects of my gardening as a battle against nature. A campaign to be won against slugs, greenfly, caterpillars but I have realised today that I am the one upsetting the balance.'

This kind of comment gladdens my heart because converts are worth their weight in gold!

Or, on the occasion when the MG Owners Club arrived with forty vintage cars: 'I'm no gardener but this place is so quiet and peaceful that it restores my spirits.'

Gardens can be havens for people as well as wildlife.

There was also humour in the form of the lady who unexpectedly came across the moss-covered classic statue in the centre of a conifer circle, saw the figure was scantily clad, clasped a hand over her eyes and said, 'Oh my goodness!' before scurrying off. Or the man who informed me that the tulip tree growing alongside the sunroom 'would be a problem for me in forty or fifty years or so'. I wish!

My favourite concerned the rambling rose bordering the patio. This vigorous, highly scented rambler is called Rambling Rector and the cuttings strike so easily that it is now all over the plot – in the hedgerows, covering old tree stumps, alongside the lakes and in fact almost anywhere that there was once a space. One elderly visitor was admiring the profusion of blooms and taking in the wonderful scent when she said, 'That is a gorgeous rose. I have one in my garden but I have always been curious as to why it is called Randy Rector. Have you any idea?'

'No,' I said, smiling, 'though as you can see from our garden, it does seem to get around a bit!'

Of course regulating the number of visitors to a wildlife sanctuary has to be a major consideration because maintenance of undisturbed areas is a must for the sustainability of any habitat. Parts of Seskinore Forest, which at that time were rich in all manner of birdlife and mammals, were opened to the public a few years ago. It has since turned into a popular venue for cyclists, dog walkers, horse riders, joggers and walkers – and the wildlife has moved out as people have moved in. Accessible country parks are obviously a good thing but their use does come at a cost to any existing wildlife – a lesson that a private garden such as ours should take care to heed.

The creation of our garden has also given me cause to think differently about one of my longest-standing interests: shooting.

For as long as I can remember, I have loved it. My grandparents lived in a remote part of Lincolnshire where, in those days, farms were chemical free and where wildlife of all kinds was abundant. Every school holiday I would stay with them and it seemed natural and normal to go out with the dog and gun. I am sure my limited successes had little effect on the populations of rabbits, partridge or pigeons. Even then, the sport was about much more than getting something for the pot.

Of course getting a plump pheasant or newly arrived woodcock was a joy, and cooking them in the simplest way possible did provide some of the best eating ever, but that was not the primary reason I ventured out. Shooting gave me a reason to get out and renew a connection with the wild places, to find solitude in quiet corners, and to enjoy the varied landscapes. It also gave me a reason to observe, close up, wildlife that many people ignored or overlooked. For me, just being out on the land was magical, and one of the real thrills was seeing the life of the woods and fields, and wondering about what roamed around them when I wasn't there.

However, starting out on our wildlife project in the early days and finding the countryside bereft of wildlife set alarm bells ringing. The more I learned of the devastation that has occurred across the land the more I felt that conservation now had to take precedence over sport. Early in 2004 I was sitting by one of the new lakes watching a duck lead six newly hatched ducklings through the reeds when I had what can only be described as a 'road to Damascus' moment, or a 'poacher turned gamekeeper' conversion, and I have never really enjoyed shooting since.

I felt I had to promote the notion of care of the countryside and its flora and fauna, and looked at ways, beyond our development of the wildlife area, to try to do this. Persuasion rather than confrontation seemed more likely to change minds so I wrote a book about shooting that encouraged followers of the sport to become 'green guns' – putting forward the idea that it was possible to enjoy good sport at the same time as protecting the countryside and the species under threat. I also began writing monthly columns for various shooting magazines that promoted notions of habitat protection, enhancement of the countryside by planting woodland or meadows, and the need for action against the continued decline of our traditional wildlife.

The motivation for writing this book was in a way a continuation of the same theme of conservation, preservation of habitat, halting the decline of wildlife and valuing our countryside. It is true that we also wanted a written record of the project for future generations and hope, in addition, that this account may go some way towards satisfying the interest many of the visiting gardeners have shown in the project.

Creation of this garden has brought other bonuses. I am now seventy-six and Rosemary is sixty-eight but we are both fit. True, not quite so sprightly as we once were, but still active and mobile and much of this we put down to the demands of the garden. There is always a task, always a reason to put on our work clothes and get some exercise, and always the temptation to stroll around the woodland paths or meadows to take the air and observe the daily comings and goings of the creatures that live here. Rosemary still runs and attends gym and Pilates classes to keep in trim, but I prefer the 'green gym', which doesn't have running machines, fitness equipment or sweating bodies, but still demands physical exertion and stamina. The outdoor exercise is so fulfilling and furthermore, at the end of a tiring day, it is very satisfying to see the results of one's labours rather than simply finishing up with a wet towel!

In 2017, exercise and the demands of the garden got us through an unexpectedly troubling time. We have always been great supporters of the Woodland Trust, not just because they helped us design and plant the nine acres of new woodland, but because we believe wholeheartedly in their vision of a country rich in woods and trees, for animals and for people to enjoy. So when the Trust approached us to open the garden as a fundraiser we readily agreed. The trouble was – as everyone who has ever run an 'open garden' day will know – that when visitors are on their way, what is perfectly acceptable in the normal run of things suddenly becomes unacceptable. The garden shed needed another coat of paint, the formal hedges needed tidying, the gravel had to be raked and a hundred other tasks finished before the big day. Jonus and Pavel, two Moldovan gardeners, were trimming the laurels and working down the to-do list when the bombshell hit. I was diagnosed with the first stages of prostate cancer and would need twenty consecutive sessions of radiotherapy in the run-up to our open day. The consultant was very optimistic that the condition could be sorted out but warned that the treatment often resulted in extreme tiredness. In the event, the cancer team in Altnagelvin was superb and having an incentive to get out into the garden every afternoon after the treatment seemed to overcome the predicted fatigue. Gardening with a purpose raises the spirit and I am sure that if I had sat around or gone to bed during this period, I would have been more down and gloomy.

The approach of a garden open day also provided yet more proof of another very pleasing aspect of the project that we had not anticipated. Rosemary and I have been astounded by the interest and support we have had from our many neighbours and friends. From day one, it was as if they we are all stirred by some instinctive desire to stop the devastation of our wildlife and get involved with our project. True to form, once the date for the open day was announced, offers of help came from all directions.

Rosemary's brother, Kevin, offered the huge space in front of his repair garage as a temporary car park. Our niece's boyfriend dug out a new path from the car park to the rear of our property. A friend, Pat, agreed to provide the tea and coffee, and our sons Ed and Matt, and daughter-in-law, Catriona, sorted out the cakes and scones. Grandchildren Joe and Izzy would be there to sell books. It was to be a full team effort!

During the preparations there were many generous acts but one in particular stands out. Brian, the father of Shane (who built the house), came up to repair the timber veranda on the wildlife-watching hut. He has completed many tasks over the years and has become a invaluable supporter – always ready to get involved if things need to be repaired or replaced. He can be forthright: 'That walkway we built from old pallets over the corner of the lake is past its prime. We don't want anyone going into the water.'

He rebuilt it.

'The diving board in the large lake is beginning to rot. I'll strengthen it.'

It was soon perfect.

At the bottom end of the three-lake system, the water leaves our property and rejoins the stream flowing down the valley. To prevent erosion during heavy rainfall, we positioned a slope of very large rocks at the exit and the water cascades down these into the waterway beyond. Crossing these boulders can be tricky if the weather is wet and the rocks slippery so I suggested to Brian that we would need to build a plank bridge before the open day. I had nightmare visions of heaps of pensioners with broken limbs lying at the foot of the waterfall and claims coming in thick and fast!

As we chatted I happened to say to Brian that I had always loved this corner of the garden, where the lake is dark and still, and the bamboo makes beautiful patterns on the surface. 'I've always thought it would be the perfect spot to build a copy of Monet's bridge near Paris.'

I went on to explain that the artist had a garden, far more exotic than ours, with water lilies and a distinctive bridge and that he had painted pictures of the spot many times.

'Do you have a photograph of it?' asked Brian.

'Yes, but actually building the thing is only a pipe dream. It's a curved bridge and would probably be far too complicated to construct.'

Back at the house I printed a picture of the bridge from the internet and Brian studied it without saying anything. Three days later he was back.

'Are you free tomorrow? I've built the bridge in the workshop and all we need to do now is assemble it.'

So there it was. Shane dug the footings, Brian jointed the structure, Rosemary painted the new timber and I cleared the brambles and planted some *Gunnera manicata*, *Fatsia japonica*, some irises and a range of different rodgersia in the hope that the corner would eventually have a slightly exotic feel. It looked wonderful!

Establishing water lilies proved a bit more problematic. We had always thought that the water at the end of the smallest lake, near to where we were building the bridge, was no more than three feet deep so decided to plant one water lily to make sure that it would survive the slightly peaty water. I donned salmon fishing waders and gingerly slithered down through the reeds to begin the planting. Unfortunately – for me and the lilies – the water was up to my chest and the lilies would not grow at that depth so we had to come up with a new plan. I decided we need something to lessen the depth so drove down to the municipal tip and retrieved an old plastic, three-foot-high laundry basket. We filled the bottom with several large stones and topped it up with soil before planting the first water lily at the recommended depth.

We had just stood back to congratulate ourselves on a job well done when our old Labrador, Willow, decided it was time to take her daily swim. She eased herself gently into the water, sailed gracefully out and caught her belly on the new water lily container. Elderly she might be, but she is still a very strong dog and a few hefty kicks from her back legs soon cleared the obstacle and sent it down into the peaty depths. Luckily more wader work and probing with a garden rake soon located the sunken item and after much pulling and tugging we were able to reassemble everything. This corner may not yet resemble Monet's glorious garden but we now have the bridge, have begun the planting and next year, if Willow stays clear, we should have our first flowering water lily!

Helpers and volunteers have rallied to help with our project in all kinds of ways. When parents from the local GAA club asked if they could escort forty of their children through the woodlands on Halloween night, neighbours Mary and Molly instantly set about transforming the courtyard and walkways into a ghostly experience. It worked brilliantly, and also gave us the opportunity to spread the word about tree planting and conservation to local children and their parents. Beyond this, we are increasingly beginning to notice a greater awareness of the need for habitat protection and the care of the local wildlife across our immediate area. It is impossible to quantify, but we get the feeling from talking to neighbours that the local boglands are now being seen differently and are mentioned as places worth preserving. There are other signs of a change in mindset as quads no longer wreck the woodland and you can spot bird feeders in almost every back garden. Our neighbour intends to plant twenty-seven acres of native trees and the local GAA club is thinking of developing a wildlife walk through the woods and farmlands surrounding their pitches. It is all very encouraging.

Sadly there do not seem to have been any significant changes to farming practices, which continue to pollute habitats with severe impacts on biodiversity. Slurry and chemicals still rain down, single farm payments still require the chopping back of hedges and, despite media campaigns in the local newspapers and on television, carcasses are still regularly dumped into ditches and rivers. Indeed the agricultural pollution of our local streams, which sometimes completely destroys the ecosystems, seems to happen annually. Although it now makes the media, there is usually only a trivial fine for the perpetrator and the event is soon forgotten.

Misuse of our rivers to the detriment of ecosystems is not always the fault of agricultural practices but can also be down to widespread disrespect for our environment. After a recent flood virtually every tree and bush along our local riverbanks was festooned with all manner of rubbish, much of which clung like shredded flags to the bank-side vegetation. High water marks along the course of the streams showed a normal trail of natural debris, such as broken twigs and reeds, but laced through this were hundreds of plastic bottles, carry-out food containers and all of the other disposable rubbish from our throwaway society. It was true that farm litter, in the form of black polythene sheets that once held silage, was also in evidence, and in several places the carcasses of sheep and calves lay rotting. It is possible, of course, that these animals had finished up in the flood by accident but in all cases any traceable markings had been removed indicating that somewhere upstream they had been deliberately dumped into the waterways.

Familiarity can blind us to reality – perhaps we have become so used to rubbish along the banks of our rivers or our roadsides that we now just don't see it. Some years ago my wife and I were working in the mountains of Transylvania. A tourist board representative explained their plans to increase visitors to the region and, in particular, their desire to attract anglers to the rivers and streams. Rosemary looked over the bridge of the picturesque town where we were staying, saw the sea of plastic which adorned every bankside bush and said, in her usual outspoken way, 'The area is beautiful but your river is filthy. No one in their right mind would want to come here.' The tourist board people were clearly offended – but came to her the following day and agreed she was right. They said they had stopped noticing how bad it was so the next day they were instigating an urgent clean-up campaign. Our dream is that everyone will begin to appreciate the true natural beauty on this island and dispose of their litter and farm waste responsibly. Until this happens, perhaps regular clean-up campaigns of our own pieces of countryside are the next best thing.

However there are local converts. A few years ago, one local farmer was asking me about planting native trees in corners of his land when four lapwings rose from a field. I was really excited to see them and explained that breeding populations of the birds had been devastated in Ireland in recent years. Drainage schemes, conversion of permanent pasture to silage, insecticides and the change to autumn sowing of grain have put the lapwing in real trouble and populations have fallen by 70 per cent.

'There have always been one or two about on those lower pastures and I like the sound they make,' the farmer remarked.

'Spring sowing gives them the habitat they need to breed but since they nest on the ground, predation by foxes and feral cats can be deadly.'

'I'll ask one of my sons to keep an eye on them,' he said thoughtfully.

By 2017 the flock numbered over thirty birds.

Another neighbour about a mile away phoned to say he had seen a strange yellow bird in the hedgerow at the rear of his house. It turned out to be a yellowhammer – scarce in these parts for many years and another casualty of changing farming methods but perhaps making a comeback.

There is still a long way to go. Luckily increased scientific research is beginning to provide hard evidence that may change future policy and practice. The State of Nature 2016 report, which was drawn up by fifty of the UK's leading conservation groups, said that wildlife across these islands is losing the battle against intensive agriculture, stating that 123 farmland species are now facing extinction and many more are at serious risk.

Blame for this crisis was placed firmly at the door of the EU, with its common agricultural policy and its system of subsidies that leaves little room for wildlife and is driving many species to extinction. Not everyone agrees of course. One Northern Irish MP stood up in parliament in November 2017 and argued that the ban on shooting raptors should be lifted because they were responsible for the decline of songbirds. Ill informed, scientifically nonsensical – but symptomatic of an attitude that promotes enduring myths in order to detract from the truth that many aspects of modern farming need to change. The grey partridge, already gone in Northern Ireland, is down by 92 per cent in Britain; the skylark down by 60 per cent; and there has been an alarming fall in the number of farmland birds since the 1970 count.

Writing reports to raise awareness is of course vital but some practical action must then follow across the land if our threatened species are to be assisted. Wildlife reserves and dedicated conservation areas are essential but they are, in reality, zoos without bars and will do little to impact on the hundreds of acres across the land that have become rural deserts. The efforts we have made over the years have already shown that creating more supportive habitats can begin to change things and challenge a culture that meekly accepts an inevitable decline amongst our native species. There must be many pockets of land across Ireland and the UK where, with effort and minimal cost, a more favourable environment for our native species could be created and maintained. Tree planting in odd corners, leaving field margins of wild flowers and allowing hedgerows to thicken and grow need not adversely affect modern farming, but doing this does require a huge change to the current mindset.

With hindsight, we look at the demise of the passenger pigeon in North America a hundred years ago and ask how was it possible that massive populations went from billions to zero in so short a time. Why was the most abundant bird in North

America hunted to extinction and why did so many people show such disregard and let this happen? Was it indifference, greed or lack of awareness that allowed this wildlife crime to take place? What are the lessons we should learn from this sorry episode? To a lesser degree, something similar is happening in our own backyard.

It is a bleak picture but it can and must be changed. Fortunately most parts of Ireland have not been subject to the level of agricultural intensity that exists in farming areas in England but the unprecedented building boom of a few years ago has meant that in many parts of the country there is much less undisturbed open space, fewer thick hedgerows, far less meadowland and much-reduced wetlands. As we noted earlier, the Northern Ireland statistics are like those across the rest of these islands and are alarming in terms of conservation: 95 per cent of wild flower meadows have gone; 50 per cent of ancient lowland woods; 60 per cent of lowland heaths; 50 per cent of traditional orchards; over 70 per cent of raised boglands. Little wonder that many of our traditional native species have already disappeared or are in serious decline. Obviously it is beyond the power of individuals to arrest the overall loss of habitat, but at the micro level we should all be doing something. However small our plots, however limited our knowledge and however tight our budgets we can all make an effort and, in the end, this will have a positive impact.

We set out fourteen years ago to try to create a wildlife-friendly habitat that would be sustainable and that would attempt to turn the clock back. With minimal expertise and little spare money we were undoubtedly naive and overly optimistic, but commitment, enthusiasm and self-belief can overcome most things and the end result has been hugely satisfying. Of course with luck the area will keep developing, keep maturing and will continue to attract further permanent residents.

What will happen to our dream in the future? Who knows?

Our three sons and their wives have lives elsewhere so our land will probably be sold, hopefully to a buyer who will value the wildlife habitat that is now here. Perhaps it will pass on to someone who will love the solitude and peace of the place and who has the passion for wildlife that we have. Ideally a kindred spirit, an enthusiastic conservationist who will take the place to the next stage and safeguard it in the future. We would hate it to eventually fall victim to developers as we have seen happen to many of our treasured landscapes over the past twenty years – because as the old saying goes, 'once it's gone, it's gone!'

We both have a horror of this happening, perhaps because we have seen it so many times. In my youth one of my favourite haunts was part of an old country estate. Rhododendrons and azaleas cloaked the sides of a narrow valley and in spring when they were in bloom, the place was truly spectacular. Oaks, pines and redwoods framed the view on the higher slopes and a rutted farm track meandered like a stream between the spurs before finally disappearing into the laurels at the foot of the slope. It was staggeringly beautiful and a perfect spot to relax and let the world go by. Sadly, a town bypass was carved through the valley, the rhododendrons were ripped out, the slopes terraced and a modern industrial complex developed. Two giant redwoods, looking totally incongruous amid the plastic and concrete of the hotels and conference centres are virtually all that remain of the old estate. They stand on some raised ground, towering above the new buildings, seeming to cast a disapproving eye over what now lies beneath them. You can almost feel them asking 'What price progress?' as they gaze down.

As beginners in the whole process of conservation and the encouragement of all forms of wildlife, we have come to realise that enthusiasm and self-belief is the key to success. Even after fourteen years, we are still beginners. We do now have some understanding of which types of habitats will hold wildlife, which kinds of plants will suit the widest range of insects, and which have been so selectively bred and hybridised that they will attract nothing, but we are still finding our way. We have come to accept that there will always be some tensions between the expectations of traditional gardening and the promotion of wildlife, but that we can overcome most of these issues by following different practices or changing our mindset. If we can learn to live with nibbled foliage on the hostas by remembering that the slugs will in turn provide food for the hedgehogs and thrushes, life in the garden becomes much less stressful. If we know the caterpillars on the cabbage will feed a brood of young birds rather than worrying about the loss of a few leaves, the world feels different. If we can accept that not all parts of the garden need to be manicured and neat, and that undisturbed, unkempt areas are vital for many species, the to-do list diminishes. Salvation lies in actions that help rather than hinder, in collaboration rather than conflict, and trying to adhere to the core belief that the preservation of all wildlife matters.

Every year that goes by sees greater maturity in the design and structure of the garden. A natural harmony seems to have emerged amongst the trees and shrubs, which now makes things look as if the plantings were all carefully planned in a professional, systematic way. We of course know that the reality was often very different, with plants pushed in wherever we had a space. Luckily much of this ad hoc approach has worked well and there is interest and surprise along the various pathways and walks. However what really brings the garden to life are the many birds, animals and insects that have made this their home and the fact that the majority are no longer disturbed by our presence. Walking by wild creatures without them becoming unduly alarmed is a wonderful privilege and makes all of our efforts seem truly worthwhile.

Over the years we have come to realise that wildlife gardens are different. They look different, sound different, and are magical and alive. In creating them we can feel we have made some small contribution towards preserving what we have. We now have our own 'bee-loud glade' with a dawn chorus that, in the spring and summer, is truly spectacular. If two total amateurs can achieve this turnaround then anyone can. It is a question of changing the way we think about gardening and wildlife and taking action rather than wringing our hands and sitting back. We set out fourteen years ago with an improbable dream but, in our small way, we have managed to make a difference. In order to sustain our country's wildlife we must seed our meadows, build our ponds, plant our woodlands and rethink our gardening practices. Committed people can change the world. We must be prepared to put in more than we take out. It is well worth the effort!